TIMBUKTU ACADEMY'S U-TURN

Implementing Systemic Organizational Change in an African-Centered Academy

All Children Deserves a Quality Education

By: Bernard F. Parker Jr.,
Brenda A. Cunningham-Parker,
and Warrington S. Parker Jr.

BALBOA.PRESS

A DIVISION OF HAY HOUSE

Balboa Press books may be ordered through booksellers or by contacting:

Balboa Press
A Division of Hay House
1663 Liberty Drive
Bloomington, IN 47403
www.balboapress.com
844-682-1282

ISBN: 979-8-7652-5701-2 (sc)
ISBN: 979-8-7652-5700-5 (e)

Print information available on the last page.

Balboa Press rev. date: 12/13/2024

Bernard F. Parker, Jr, CEO; Brenda A. Cunningham-Parker, BA, MFA, Educator; Warrington S. Parker, Jr. Ph D, Organizational Psychologist.

CONTENTS

DEDICATIONS

Dedication by Bernard F. Parker Jr.:

To my parents, Bernard F. Parker Sr. and Rebecca Dais Parker, whose unwavering guidance has inspired me to give back to the community and support the underserved. Additionally, I dedicate this work to Malkia Brantuo, the co-founder of the Academy, and to all the teachers who were instrumental in establishing the school. Special thanks go to the dedicated teachers, both past and present, who continue to shape the minds of our students.

Dedication by Brenda A. Cunningham-Parker:

To my mother, Clover Bell-Santiago, who, as a single mother, instilled in me the value of education and inspired me to be a child advocate. Her unwavering dedication to protecting the rights and comfort of children with loving care continues to be my guiding principle.

Dedication by Warrington S. Parker Jr.:

To my parents, Pauline M. Dais Parker and Warrington S. Parker Sr., whose enduring love has instilled in me a profound appreciation for all humanity and a deep respect for my African American heritage. Their teachings have imbued me with the value of education and the importance of sharing my knowledge with young students.

FOREWORD

This book explores an African-Centered Academy in Detroit and its enduring success in providing quality education to African American students. The first nine chapters are written by me, Bernard F. Parker Jr., the CEO, while the remaining chapters are authored by Brenda A. Cunningham-Parker and Warrington S. Parker Jr., Ph.D. Even as other institutions have closed, I established one of the first African-Centered schools in Detroit under a five-year charter from the Detroit Public Schools. By 2007-2008, I began noticing significant challenges, and by 2009, it was clear that the Academy needed a new direction. Consequently, I approved a turnaround process.

I enlisted Brenda A. Parker, an educator with a BA in education, an MFA, and former head of private independent schools in Los Angeles, to contribute her educational leadership as the school principal. I firmly believe that the success of a school turnaround is largely dependent on the principal's instructional leadership. Brenda's ability to stay current with state-of-the-art educational practices, her effective management skills, and her adeptness at working with staff, students, parents, and boards of directors were crucial to our success.

Warrington S. Parker Jr., PhD, an organizational psychologist, was also enlisted. His experience in designing innovative high-performance, high-commitment team-based work systems at Rockwell Corporation contributed significantly to our efforts.

The success of this process resulted from the blend of our diverse skills. As a community organizer, founder and CEO of the Academy, and an elected Wayne County Commissioner, I also brought my expertise to the table.

This book was written primarily to celebrate the school's success and, secondly, to demonstrate how a school like the Academy can thrive in an educational desert. It aims to inspire educators and educational leaders. School principals, administrators, teachers, consultants, and board members will find valuable insights in this book.

Through strong leadership, dedicated teaching, innovative programs, and a strong support network, all schools can provide students with the quality education they deserve.

INTRODUCTION

This book chronicles the journey of an inner-city, urban, African-centered, Detroit Public Charter School that I co-founded. It explores its inception, growth, maturity, decline, and eventual rebirth. Timbuktu Academy of Science and Technology is situated on the East Side of Detroit, Michigan. The process of educating students at Timbuktu Academy fulfills the universal human rights of providing quality education for all students.

African American students are often denied a quality education due to systemic racism. The Academy was established to counteract this inequity by offering quality education specifically for African American students. Every student at the Academy is given the opportunity to achieve their intellectual potential and become self-supporting, peaceful, contributing citizens of our global society. Additionally, students are taught to be knowledgeable and proud of their African American heritage, traditions, and contributions to the economic well-being and culture of the United States.

A school like the Academy is vitally important in a Black community that lacks quality educational institutions because it provides a beacon of hope and a pathway to success for its students. In areas where educational resources are scarce, the Academy serves as a crucial platform for academic excellence, cultural affirmation, and community empowerment. It offers a tailored educational experience that acknowledges and addresses the unique challenges faced by Black students, fostering an environment where they can thrive academically and personally. By promoting high standards of learning and instilling a sense of pride in their cultural heritage, Timbuktu not only elevates the individual prospects of its students but also contributes to the broader socio-economic development of the community.

Through dedicated leadership and teaching, innovative programs, and a strong support network, the school becomes a cornerstone for building future leaders and change-makers within the community

The Academy's primary objective is to provide a high-quality education for African American students, offering them a safe haven and an environment conducive to learning, supported by a caring staff.

Every student attending the Academy deserves the best possible education, and the dedicated staff strives to provide it. This has been our unwavering vision through all the ups and downs of the Academy's existence.

This is a story about the Academy's rich history, encompassing its successes, challenges, the impact of location changes, growth, issues with teacher certifications, and schoolwide assessment results. It also highlights the Academy's value to the community. This school serves "underserved, deserving" students living in a poverty-level community, with many children experiencing chronic toxic stress conditions that adversely affect their brain development and learning

An article written by Warrington and Brenda Parker for the Academy's teachers and staff, titled "The Effects of Chronic Stress on Student Learning," is included in *Appendix E*. Another article, "The Brain at School and Work," written for faculty and staff, can be found in *Appendix D*.

In writing this book, I collaborated with two other authors to illuminate the oasis-like environment we provided for the students and the pride we felt in operating an African American-centered Academy. We also highlighted the growth of our students, parent involvement, and the services the school provided to the community. Furthermore, we detail the efforts employed to turn around the school before it declined beyond repair thus ensuring the continued provision of quality education for the students attending the Academy today.

CHAPTER I
HISTORY OF THE FOUNDING OF THE AFRICAN-CENTERED ACADEMY

The inception of the Academy traces back to 1989 in Detroit, Michigan Timbuktu was established with the intent of providing quality African-centered learning experiences for children and families in the surrounding African American communities. The Academy focused on building Black students' confidence and self-esteem by integrating the state-required curriculum with education about African American culture, ideals, values, and history.

The Community of the Academy

The Academy is located on the east side of Detroit, in a community where the once vibrant businesses that lined the major streets have noticeably disappeared, reflecting the broader decline of the city. Yet, signs of restoration are emerging, as newly constructed homes are sporadically scattered throughout the surrounding streets.

The abandoned and boarded-up houses that once littered the perimeter along Canfield and Montclair no longer stand. In their place, there are now empty, vacant spaces—spaces that, much like the minds of the young children who enter the Academy each day, long to be nurtured, developed, and filled, but never wasted.

The students who walk to school often find themselves walking in the streets rather than on the sidewalks to avoid wild dogs or predators lurking in the abandoned houses. They must also be vigilant to avoid encounters with gang members who might assault them for their money. This book is about educating those students in high-poverty communities, with the Academy serving as an oasis where they can learn and grow.

Schools in high-poverty areas do not achieve high academic progress by making one or two changes, nor by merely reacting to problems as they arise. School leaders cannot ignore the impact of poverty and drugs on the students they serve. High-performing schools in high-poverty communities confront these barriers to student achievement and must structure their programs and instruction to eradicate, or at least minimize, the effects of poverty on student performance. This is in a neighborhood where calling the police often does not elicit a response.

While schools cannot eradicate poverty, they can provide interventions to address its impact on students' brains and their learning. When students entered the Academy, they felt safe, surrounded by loving and caring teachers and staff. The Academy was started at Operation Get Down, a community organization that I also co-founded.

1

CHAPTER II
AFRICAN CENTERED UJIMA. EARLY CHILDHOOD DEVELOPMENT CENTER

The education of African American children began with Operation Get Down's (OGD) "Ujima," the Early Childhood Development Center, in 1989. Operation Get Down (OGD) was located on the East Side of Detroit at Gratiot Avenue and Harper Street, the neighborhood where I grew up.

Ujima, which means "collective work and responsibility," emphasizes the development and preservation of Black communities. It serves as a framework for addressing the problems of others as your own and challenges practitioners to collectively solve issues affecting the Black community. See the *Appendix A* for more details.

The mission of the Early Childhood Development Center was to improve the quality of life for families in the Detroit community, with particular emphasis on African American families, through initiatives that advocated for positive change, education to uplift and empower, improved economic conditions, and strategies for self-determination.

Operation Get Down, Inc. (OGD) was a non-profit, community-based agency serving metro Detroiters since 1971. Centrally located at the intersection of Harper and Gratiot Avenues, OGD has been a mainstay of the Eastside community for more than four decades. Born from the community-organization movement in the 1970s, OGD is a true grassroots success story.

While many grassroots organizations of the 1970s have come and gone, Operation Get Down has grown into a million-dollar, CARF-accredited United Way-member agency serving more than 35,000 people each year. OGD is proud of its neighborhood heritage and equally proud of its proven ability to evolve and remain flexible in an increasingly complex funding and service-delivery environment.

Through ever-changing times, the hallmark of OGD's continued success and viability has been its strong track record for identifying and responding to current and emerging community needs.

During the 1980s, OGD became synonymous with food distribution to the community's most needy citizens.

Bernard Parker

I, along with Barry Hankerson, founded Operation Get Down (OGD). Barry Hankerson was a community organizer from New York. As two inspired young community leaders, we ultimately established OGD, where I served as Executive Director for over 30 years.

Under the leadership of E. Malkia Brantuo and myself, OGD initiated the African-centered school that later became Timbuktu Academy. The early childhood school we started was named Ujima.

CHAPTER III
PARENTS REQUEST

From Pre-School Academy to The Next Phase

At Operation Get Down (OGD), even before establishing the school, we consistently promoted quality education for children and created African-centered programs for the East Side community. When we founded the preschool academy, it quickly gained recognition as one of the best in the city due to the program's success.

Parents' Request: Ujima's school parents wanted the next phase of their children's educational experiences to be as rewarding as the preschool academy had been. From the desires of parents and community members, Timbuktu Academy of Science and Technology was established.

At OGD, we learned that despite the community's designation as the poorest in Detroit, parents and caregivers consistently pursued the best educational options for their children. Parents sought small class sizes, individualized instruction, opportunities for exposure through field trips, diverse materials, committed teachers, and innovative educational approaches—similar to those found in affluent public academies.

In 1996, with a loan and a strong commitment to making it happen, E. Malkia Brantuo and I sought to meet the needs of the parents by opening the doors of Timbuktu Academy of Science and Technology. However, after only four months in operation, despite our continued commitment to providing this essential education to African American students, the Academy's doors temporarily closed due to financial constraints.

One of the key reasons I believe the Academy has been operating since 1989 has been a determination, to realize its vision, of providing the eastside with a quality education for the children. The financial management fell to me. I supervised this throughout the many ups and downs never giving up and adjusting when necessary. I had a dedicated staff that worked for minimum wages. . Many other African American centered schools failed because of poor financial management. not able to manage through their rocky journeys.

Through my and E. Malkia Brantuo, concerted efforts we accomplished a winning feat. The African Centered Academy, K-12 school received a five-year Charter, from the Detroit Public Schools. A first in Detroit.

The Academy Granted a 5-Year Charter

Our persistence was rewarded on September 23, 1997, when the Detroit Board of Education granted us a 5-year charter as a public K-12 charter African American Centered Academy. To grow the Academy went through trials and tribulation, but always provided a quality education for the students for over twenty-three years

In its inaugural year, 1997-1998, the Academy served grades K-3, adding one grade each year until reaching the 8th grade. The Academy of Science and Technology initially enrolled 67 students, with 58 certified for attendance by Wayne RESA, the Intermediate Academy District to which the Academy belonged. These certified students required more personalized attention from the school to emphasize the importance of attendance and to develop intervention barrier-reduction plans. The interventions aims to remove attendance barriers for students at higher risk of chronic absenteeism.

Growing Enrollment

The Academy began in a small facility at 9980 Gratiot on Detroit's east side but soon had to purchase commercial trailers to accommodate the growing enrollment. The leadership successfully employed qualified teachers who not only lived by but also practiced the philosophy and were dedicated to developing an African-centered curriculum. Due to the Academy's unique curriculum, it was able to secure Provisional Teaching Certification from the Michigan Department of Education for all staff.

The Academy grew to serve over 150 K-8 children and attracted students from across the city of Detroit. Parents selected the Academy because they believed in its approach and wanted the best education for their children. The Academy enjoyed a high level of parental involvement and support for their children's education.

Over the years, the Academy consistently provided quality education to the children it served. Each year, the students' academic achievement improved. In 2002, the Academy received the State of Michigan Golden Apple Award, recognizing that over 90% of thestudents passed the state MEAP test.

The years 2001 to 2008 brought many awards and recognitions for the Academy. These included the Golden Apple Award for significant improvement in MEAP test scores during the school years 2001-2002 and 2003-2004, and the Skillman grant award for achievement on the MEAP in 2006 and 2007.

During the following years, the Academy received numerous grants, including funding from the Skillman Foundation, Youth Sports and Recreation, Comerica Bank, Marygrove College, and the Beaumont Foundation. Several teachers received statewide and national recognition for their dedication and excellence in teaching.

From its beginnings, the Academy was a community school born out of and responsive to the needs of the community. Unlike many charter schools that drew their population from expansive and broad areas of the city and tri-county area, more than 75% of the Academy's student population resided within the 48214 zip, code in which the school was located, with the remaining population residing in adjacent zip codes 48213 and 48215, each having a comparable poverty level.

At some point, I was faced with challenges regarding the teacher's certifications. This challenge plagued the Academy's teaching staff and affected teaching and student learning.

CHAPTER IV
TEACHING CERTIFICATIONS

In 2007, the Michigan Department of Education rescinded the Academy's use of Provisional Teacher Certification, necessitating the replacement of 70% of the teaching staff within a year. This development posed a significant setback to the objectives of the African-Centered Academy.

In 2008, due to the prohibitive costs of renovating the Doyle facility at Gratiot and Harper, the Academy relocated to its current address at 10800 E. Canfield.

The Pursuit of Certified Teachers

The Academy's pursuit of state-certified teachers resulted in a shift away from its foundational African-centered principles. These principles emphasized hiring staff who not only embodied and practiced African-centered values but also had a deep understanding of methodologies specifically designed for teaching African American children, ensuring that their educational experience was firmly rooted in their cultural heritage.

Previously, the Academy successfully hired qualified teachers with state provisional teaching certifications who were dedicated to centering education on the students' cultural heritage and contributing to the development of an African-centered curriculum. The Michigan Department of Education granted Provisional Teaching Certificates to all staff due to the Academy's unique curriculum.

Under these provisions, the Academy expanded to serve over 150 K-8 students, attracting families from across Detroit. Parents chose the Academy for its distinctive educational approach, which resulted in high levels of parental involvement and support in their children's education.

However, after significant staff turnover, the institution lost many of its core principles, leading to a shift in both the student population and parental involvement.

Despite these changes, the Academy continued to uphold a cultural environment aligned with the original principles of the Council of Independent Black Institutions (CIB). While some original cultural practices were maintained, the Academy also provided a supportive learning environment with small classrooms, qualified teachers, and nutritious meals for students. It remained a pioneer in implementing an African-centered DPS charter school.

CHAPTER V
THE ACADEMY AS A PIONEER

DPS Five Year Charter for an African-Centered School

Under the DPS charter, the Academy, implemented an African-Centered educational approach based on the teachings of notable Black scholars such as Asa G. Hilliard III, Ed.D., and Kofi Lomotey. These scholars researched and advocated for African-Centered teaching methods. Additionally, the Academy utilized an African-Centered curriculum developed by the Portland School System for reading and social studies, along with the rituals established by the Council of Independent Black Institutions (CIBI). The founders of the Academy firmly believed in the value of African-Centered education.

This approach enables African American students to view the world with Africa at the center, incorporating instructional and curricular strategies that shift students' worldviews and reorient their values and actions accordingly. According to Temple University Professor Molefi Asante, in his 1980 work *Afrocentricity: The Theory of Social Change*, "African-Centered approaches prioritize the interests and concerns of people of African descent. These approaches center their narratives in various forms, such as books, films, classrooms, and visual art. Unlike a Eurocentric model, an African-Centered model emphasizes community over individualism. For example, Black history is often taught from a Eurocentric perspective, highlighting individual achievements against societal barriers but failing to adequately examine how historical figures impacted their communities."

I was particularly interested in Afrocentric teaching and learning within the Academy's classrooms, situating current efforts and offerings within the broader historical struggle for equity for African-descended peoples in the United States. Many activists, scholars, and groups have long recognized the importance of raising awareness among African peoples about how racism, Eurocentricity, and racial power work to resist white supremacy faced by Africans in the Diaspora.

Afrocentric Education

Afrocentric education is a pedagogical approach designed to empower people of the African diaspora with educational methods that align with the cultural assumptions prevalent in their communities. A fundamental premise is that many Africans have been subjugated by limiting their self-awareness and indoctrinating them with ideas counterproductive to their cultures. Proponents argue that educational methods effective for one group may not necessarily educate and empower another, necessitating distinct educational priorities for Africans in specific contexts.

Philosophy

Afrocentric education aims to decolonize the African mind, a process that involves rejecting the authority of alien traditions. This concept is central to the goal of decolonization.

The Miseducation of the Negro

I read *The Miseducation of the Negro* and studied the first three African-centered schools established in Detroit before opening the Academy. In *The Miseducation of the Negro*, Carter G. Woodson coined the term "Afrocentric" to describe the systematic deprivation of African Americans' knowledge of self. Woodson believed that miseducation was the root of many problems within the African American community. He argued that if African Americans were provided with accurate knowledge and education from the start, they would not face their current challenges. Woodson contended that African Americans often valorize European culture to the detriment of their own.

The Academy was a pioneer in implementing an African-centered DPS charter school, aiming to build commitment and competency within current and future generations to support the struggle for liberation, pride, and independent thinking among African Americans.

CHAPTER VI
CONCERNS ABOUT ACADEMIC PROGRESS

Between 2006 and 2008, I became increasingly concerned about the lack of academic progress among the students at the Academy and the shift in school culture away from prioritizing effective teaching and student learning.

I observed several signs indicating that the Academy needed to change direction. These included declining state test scores, a diminished focus on student learning, decreased teaching effectiveness, and a tendency to blame parents and students for academic shortcomings. Additionally, a culture was emerging where staff members prioritized their own needs—such as arriving late or leaving early—over student learning. Despite these issues, the Academy remained committed to African-centered education.

I believe this decline was largely due to the Academy having to hire 70% of the teaching staff within a year. While these teachers were certified, many were not necessarily committed to the school's primary tenet of centering children's education on cultural information and dedicating themselves to developing an African-centered curriculum.

Changes in the community also had a negative impact. Since 2006, the neighborhood had been in further decline. Rising unemployment and foreclosure rates in Detroit critically undermined the community's financial stability. Consequently, the demand for the Academy grew as more Detroit Public Schools (DPS) closed.

The school population shifted from 65% of students whose parents selected the Academy because of its teaching philosophy to a neighborhood school where 90% of the parents sent their children to the Academy because they believed it was better than other schools in the area.

Within the three zip codes surrounding the Academy, there were two other charter schools and three DPS schools serving grades K-8. Children from low-income households, particularly those whose parents lacked transportation, were typically constrained to attending local neighborhood schools. This situation effectively limited parental choice in selecting schools for their children.

Enrolling Every Student Became a Problem

In compliance with charter school legislation, the Academy enrolled every student that applied. By the end of September, it became apparent that rival gangs had infiltrated the school. Some of the new teachers expressed concerns and apprehensions about these gang-affiliated students. Soon, the family-like, African-centered, collaborative, and peaceful environment began to erode.

To address this issue, the Academy partnered with several non-profit and government agencies to eradicate gang activity and student violence, including HOPE, Wayne County's "Scared Straight," Truancy Intervention, and others. Assemblies were conducted for students, parents, and staff to eliminate negative behavior.

From its inception, the Academy was a community school born out of and responsive to the needs of the community, with the goal of providing education for African American students and parents. Unlike many charter schools that draw their population from expansive and broad areas of the city and tri-county region, more than 75% of the Academy's current student population resided within the 48214 zip code, where the school is located. The remaining population resided in adjacent zip codes, 48213 and 48215, which have comparable poverty levels.

CHAPTER VII
THE ACADEMY'S RELOCATION ENCOUNTERS PROBLEMS

In 2008, the Academy relocated to a closed former DPS grade school building at 10800 Canfield Street due to the prohibitive costs of renovating the Doyle facility. The move coincided with the need to replace 70% of the teaching staff because of certification issues. Many of these new teachers didn't understand or practice an African-centered lifestyle. As a result, the Academy experienced a decline in student enrollment, which also led to reduced parental involvement.

While the new building on Canfield Street was larger and an improvement over the Doyle facility, the surrounding neighborhood presented a very different challenging environment. Many of the legacy parents chose not to move with the school.

After the move, a new principal was hired in 2006 with Board approval and a commitment to hiring a highly qualified staff. The Academy found itself with many new teachers, students, and parents from the surrounding neighborhood—most of whom were unfamiliar with the deeply embedded African-centered philosophy and school culture that had previously defined the school's success.

As previously mentioned, the Academy was undergoing significant changes, further alienating the remaining legacy parents. The new principal was ineffective in managing the Academy. In seeking a new direction, several areas of contention emerged. We realized our mistake in expanding too rapidly. The Academy was mandated to accept every student that applied, which negatively impacted student test scores, teaching effectiveness, school culture, and parental support.

In addition to the challenges posed by the Academy's physical relocations, I became particularly concerned when the Academy failed to consistently attain Adequate Yearly Progress (AYP). Test scores were declining, and I began to worry about the overall well-being of the Academy.

The following chart illustrates how test scores fluctuated over the years, with 2006 showing the lowest point after the move to the new location and the hiring of the new teachers.

2006--2008

Reading	3rd Grade	4th Grade	5th Grade	6th Grade	7th Grade	8th Grade
2008	55%	52%	72%	46%	45%	16%
2007	70%	83%	59%	39%	29%	61%
2006	54%	52%	55%	53%	41%	44%
Mathematics	3rd Grade	4th Grade	5th Grade	6th Grade	7th Grade	8th Grade

2008	68%	58%	72%	31%	43%	37%
2007	96%	76%	40%	24%	30%	36%
2006	66%	76%	40%	27%	15%	28%

The 2006 and 2007 MEAP scores reflected the school's state of transition. Scores for 2007 showed gains in reading across all elementary grades. Grade 4 remained constant in mathematics, while all other grades showed improvement. However, scores for middle school grades 6 and 7 decreased in reading, with grade 6 also showing a decline in mathematics. Grade 8, however, showed improvement in both mathematics and reading.

The school's October 2008 MEAP scores reflected a further loss of focus, discipline, and consistency across most grades. Grades 5, 6, and 7 showed gains in both reading and mathematics, with grade 8 showing a slight gain of 1% in mathematics. However, the gains made by grades 6 and 7 were insufficient to meet AYP (Adequate Yearly Progress) targets for middle school (54%). Grades 3 and 5 exceeded the AYP elementary target (65%) in mathematics, with grade 5 surpassing the AYP target (59%) in reading. Overall, the school had not attained AYP (Adequate Yearly Progress) as it had in the past.

Schools exist for teaching and student learning. If a school loses this focus, it will decline and eventually cease to exist. Help was sought before the Academy reached a point beyond possible turnaround.

When schools consistently fail to make AYP after previously doing so, it's crucial to evaluate the factors contributing to the decline and implement necessary changes to eliminate inhibitors and address invasive issues. I knew it was time for me to step up and take decisive actions—actions that many school leaders, often to the school's peril, hesitant to take.

CHAPTER VIII
THE NEED FOR A SCHOOL ASSESSMENT

Based on the overall decline in student academic achievement, effective teaching, and the changing school culture, I sought to assess the Academy's systems, programs, curriculum, faculty, administration, and all aspects of its operations. My intent was to use the data gathered to inform decisions about the future direction of the Academy. I believed the Academy needed to move in a new direction, but I was unsure how to achieve that.

I enlisted an experienced educator and an Organizational Psychologist to assess and obtain data that would guide our decisions about the school's future direction. Schools that have ended up in the "Graveyard of Ineffective Schools – Those That Did Not Make AYP" often failed to evaluate and take corrective steps before reaching the point of no return. Their continued operation might have been possible had they intervened earlier. Determined to avoid such a fate, I sought assistance to prevent failure.

CHAPTER IX
A TIME TO CHANGE

I understood that schools exist for teaching and student learning. If a school loses this focus, it will decline and eventually cease to exist. To prevent the Academy from reaching the point of no return, I sought help. I believed that when people in an organization unite under a common purpose, vision, or mission, success—though challenging—can be achieved with leadership and an effective change process. Recognizing that organizations, comprised of fallible human beings, inevitably become dysfunctional over time, I accepted this reality.

The Warrington Group

In 2009, I reached out to the Warrington Group, based in Sedona, AZ, to conduct an objective assessment, analysis, and evaluation of the Academy, particularly in areas needing a new direction. After their analysis, I requested recommendations. An evidence-based, multidimensional assessment approach was implemented

The two principal owners, Warrington Parker, Jr., Ph.D., and Brenda Parker, MFA, are Detroit natives from the same neighborhood as the Academy.

Warrington, a retired vice president of Rockwell Corporation—a diversified high-technology global company with forty-five billion dollars in sales—served customers in defense, electronics, aerospace, automotive, communications, and avionics. He was trained in survey feedback methodology at the University of Michigan's Institute for Social Research and developed employee questionnaires at Rockwell. Known for his research in brain-based learning and in assessing and redesigning complex, high-technology businesses, Warrington utilized a High-Performance Organization Systems design process based on Socio-Technical System design theory.

Brenda, an educator with extensive experience, served as Head of Private Independent Schools and was a turnaround leader with years of classroom experience. She worked as an administrator and principal for over twenty-five years in both public and private schools. For ten years, she evaluated and recommended improvements for California's private independent schools. Brenda's success in transforming private schools into institutions of quality and excellence in learning highlights her skills as a creative instructional leader, problem solver, and consummate educator.

In recognition of Brenda's success in increasing diversity at a private independent school in Los Angeles, a parent donated one million dollars to establish the Brenda A. Parker Legacy Fund. This fund was designed to sustain the school's diversity by providing scholarships for deserving, underserved children who wished to attend the school.

I asked Brenda and Warrington to write the following chapters from their perspectives.

CHAPTER X
THE TURNAROUND FROM WARRINGTON AND BRENDA'S PERSPECTIVES

(The following sections of the book are written by Warrington and Brenda Parker)

Our involvement with the Academy began with managing an assessment survey. Following the survey, we traveled to Detroit, Michigan, to present the results to the principal, staff, parents, and the Board of Directors. During this visit, we also conducted on-site interviews with teachers, administrators, students, and parents. This hands-on approach allowed us to understand the Academy on a more personal level and provided valuable insights into its operations.

The image below is the way the Academy looked outside when we first arrived at the Academy in 2009. Shortly after taking leadership of the school, we worked diligently to ensure that the facility remained clean and well-maintained, with highly polished floors, creating a comfortable and inviting atmosphere for students to study.

The walls were adorned with images of prominent African Americans, fostering an inspiring environment. Additionally, Bernard, the CEO, installed a fish tank, in the main hallway, and a waterfall feature with koi fish in the atrium thus, enhancing the overall ambiance.

A view of Timbuktu Academy when we first arrived. Now renamed "Obama Leadership Academy"

CHAPTER XI
FOUR-PART ACADEMY ASSESSMENT PROCESS WITH RESULTS

1. We implemented a four-part assessment process to gain a deeper understanding of the Academy and provide Bernard with recommendations for moving in a new direction.
2. We developed a confidential employee questionnaire and administered it to 100% of the staff. The scaled questionnaire, designed using a Likert-type scale, received an excellent return rate of 88%.

   - A Likert scale is a rating tool used to measure opinions, attitudes, perceptions, or behaviors. It consists of a statement or question followed by a series of five or seven answer options. Respondents select the option that best reflects their feelings about the statement or question. Because respondents are given a range of possible answers, Likert scales are effective in capturing nuanced levels of agreement or feelings on the topic
   - I had the privilege of being trained by Dr. Rensis Likert while working at the University of Michigan's Institute for Social Research in Ann Arbor. I later applied his survey feedback methodology as a change agent in the General Motors-Institute for Social Research (GM-ISR) change project and at Rockwell. We interviewed all faculty and staff members to gather their personal perceptions of the issues facing the Academy.

3. We reviewed school policies, procedures, and records to identify any areas that needed attention.
4. We interviewed a cross-section of students and parents to understand their perspectives on the Academy's challenges.

Results Indicated a Lack of and the Strength's perceived by Staff

- **Consistent Student Discipline:** Some staff reported that students roamed the halls freely, giving the impression that students were not disciplined in the school.
- **Clarity and Implementation of African-Centered Vision:** The vision, philosophy, and African American history were not clearly integrated into the curriculum and daily lessons.

- **Systematic Educational Program and Curriculum:** There was no cohesive educational program across all school levels, with little evidence of teamwork or adherence to a school-wide curriculum.
- **Knowledge of Michigan Grade Level Content Expectations (GLCEs):** Many teachers were unaware of the GLCEs, and the curriculum was not aligned with teaching strategies designed to meet these standards. In Michigan, the GLCEs provide a framework for curriculum development and instruction in key areas like math, science, and reading. Students were tested annually through the MEAP assessment to determine their mastery of the GLCEs.
- **Data-Driven Decision-Making:** There was no system in place for teachers to use data to inform their instruction.
- **Accountability Among Teachers:** Teachers often attributed students' academic and social failures to their parents/guardians, the students' backgrounds, and a lack of motivation to learn. They also blamed the poor neighborhood for the lack of resources. The possibility of student failure being a "teacher problem" was never addressed.
-
- **Innovative and Effective Teaching Strategies:** There was a lack of rigorous and relevant teaching methods. In some cases, teachers attempted to teach while seated behind their desks, with students seated in traditional rows.
- **Instructional or Curriculum Leadership:** There was no instructional or curriculum leader to help teachers stay current with educational developments or to monitor and observe instruction.
- **Data-Driven Decision-Making:** There was no system in place for teachers to use data to inform their instruction.
- **Accountability Among Teachers:** Teachers often attributed students' academic and social failures to their parents/guardians, the students' backgrounds, and a lack of motivation to learn. They also blamed the poor neighborhood for the lack of resources. The possibility of student failure being a "teacher problem" was never addressed.
- **Lack of a System's Management Strategy.** Furthermore, the administration did not seem to manage the Academy as a unified system. There appeared to be a lack of focus on academics, and some faculty members frequently resorted to angry, frustrated yelling at students.
- **Over 85% of the students were found to be below grade level in reading and math.** Teachers informed us that middle school students were not interested in taking the Michigan Educational Assessment Program (MEAP) test, which contributed to the school not making Adequate Yearly Progress (AYP) in 2008.

Strengths

- **Most of the teachers were proud to teach African-Centered curriculum.**
- **Most of the teachers believed that teaching African-Centered curriculum would increase student's motivation to improve their academy performance.**
- **Most of the teachers related well to the culture of the students, parents and community.**

The four-part assessment process provided us with a deeper, more personalized understanding of the Academy and offered clearer insights into its operations. The results indicated that the Academy faced systemic issues, suggesting that a comprehensive Turnaround Process was needed to implement changes across the entire organization.

When we arrived at the Academy to provide feedback, we were surprised to find a disorderly environment. Students were running out of the building and even jumping out of windows during a fire drill. There appeared to be no effective student discipline system in place. It seemed that students had free rein, which was undoubtedly negatively impacting both teaching and learning.

Although the current principal was academically capable, she appeared to lack the leadership skills necessary to effectively guide and support the Academy's teachers.

CHAPTER XII
PRINCIPAL RESIGNED IN 2009

After we completed the survey, we provided feedback to the staff, parents, and the Board of Directors. The Chairman of the Board, who was the husband of the principal at the time, encouraged her to resign. He announced to the board, "My wife is resigning today." We were surprised by this sudden decision.

A New Head Hired

To ensure continuity and consistency, Bernard asked Brenda Parker to lead the Academy as Principal and Superintendent of the charter school. Brenda accepted the position, and I was pleased to join her as her assistant.

After retiring from our respective careers, we made a commitment to work together in the future. Early in our marriage, we recognized that we collaborated effectively in teaching, consulting, and writing.

The article below details our beginning at Timbuktu Academy in September 2009. It was featured in Detroit's *BLAC Magazine* under the title, "New Leadership, New Direction, Renewed Focus," and includes pictures of us with students.

TIMBUKTU

NEW LEADERSHIP.
NEW DIRECTION.
RENEWED FOCUS.

Timbuktu Academy of Science and Technology, a K-8 Detroit charter school located on the city's lower eastside, has pioneered a new concept in public school education dedicated to continuous improvement through productive and positive learning experiences for every student. This is being achieved in a supportive environment that reaches and teaches the total child with high expectations for success.

A new school year brings new beginnings. With a new principal and administrative team, Timbuktu has enhanced its approach to educating students in ways that are exciting teachers, students and families. Brenda Parker, the new Timbuktu principal, brings a unique curriculum focus creating an atmosphere where students are groomed to be future leaders.

Principal Parker, or "Mama Brenda" as she is lovingly called at Timbuktu, was born and raised in Detroit and attended public schools on the eastside of the city. She began her career in education thirty years ago as a classroom teacher and was a private school principal for fourteen years.

"THROUGHOUT MY CAREER, I HAVE BEEN A PASSIONATE ADVOCATE FOR THE RIGHTS OF ALL CHILDREN TO RECEIVE THE BEST EDUCATION POSSIBLE," SAYS PRINCIPAL PARKER.

"I have returned to Detroit to give back to my community that gave me so much." Principal Parker is a graduate of the University of Michigan with a BA of Distinction in Education and attended Carnegie Mellon University in Pittsburgh, PA, where she received a master's degree.

Another new addition to the Timbuktu administrative team is native Detroiter Dr. Warrington Parker, Jr., who is married to Principal Parker. "Baba Warrington," as he is affectionately known, had a successful career in the private sector, retiring as Vice President of Organizational and Leadership Development at Rockwell Corporation. Dr. Parker holds a Ph.D. in Organizational Psychology from the University of Michigan. Together, Mama Brenda and Baba Warrington are a passionate and committed team, combining their expertise to educate children in an urban school setting.

Under the guidance and direction of Principal Parker, there are many new and positive things at Timbuktu. In the first week of school, 8th grade students asked for the bathrooms to be painted. The students approached Mama Brenda with the idea and not only did she agree to their request, she offered them an opportunity to design and paint the bathrooms. The students accepted the challenge and began a brainstorming process, organized themselves and turned a brown-walled bathroom into one with colorful walls, hand-drawn flowers and decorative accessories. "The newly designed bathroom illustrates our belief that positive self esteem is enhanced when students are given leadership opportunities," said Mama Brenda.

A "Reflection Garden" is also a new concept that Principal Parker has instituted. Over the summer, school administrators, teachers and volunteers designed and built the Reflection Garden, which features a waterfall and fish-filled pond. Students, parents and visitors are captivated by the new garden, with several students proudly commenting, "My school has a waterfall!" The Reflection Garden is a safe place where students are encouraged to reflect on their goals and dreams, as well as concerns.

Principal and Dr. Parker have combined their wealth of experience with African Centered strategies to develop what they have termed "Umoja Teams," a concept that employs best practices in business and education in a holistic approach to teaching. Teachers and staff meet regularly to plan student schedules and discuss student progress, and every staff member mentors ten students.

"When a teacher is able to make decisions, they feel a sense of fulfillment and become better teachers, everyone benefits," said Dr. Parker.

Formed in 1997, Timbuktu continues to be a leader in African Centered Education, adopting a culture that nurtures every child setting by expectations and guiding their success; they deserve nothing less! Contact Timbuktu at (313) 823-6000 or www.timbuktuacademy.org.

Timbuktu Academy
10800 E. Canfield, Detroit
(313) 823-6000
www.timbuktuacademy.org

BLACdetroit.com • SEPTEMBER 2009 • BLAC 1

My role was to assist Brenda by applying my organizational change skills, providing research-based professional development training for staff, and focusing on team-based organizations, high motivation, high performance, and high commitment organizations. I also aimed to incorporate brain-based education, highlighting the connection between the brain and student learning, and to assist with evidence-based organizational change. Meanwhile, Brenda would bring her expertise as an instructional leader and her knowledge of state-of-the-art educational systems.

CHAPTER XIII
THE ACADEMY'S TURNAROUND STRATEGY A SYSTEMS APPROACH TO CHANGE

After analyzing the assessment results, Bernard, Brenda and I concluded that the Academy needed a systems turnaround change process. Systems change, or systemic change, involves addressing the fundamental causes of problems rather than just their symptoms.

This approach transforms the underlying structures, systems, processes, staff skills, culture, reward systems, customs, mindsets, power dynamics, and policies. Unlike a problem-solving change approach that targets individual issues, a systems change strategy addresses the entire organizational system.

The Academy's organizational components in need of change included its vision, goals, strategies, structure, processes, systems, culture, staff skills, technology, leadership, and performance outcomes. Additionally, system variables included external demands from parents, Detroit Public Schools requirements, and state, county, and local regulations.

These system components are always intended to work together cohesively for the organization's success. When they fail to do so, the organization will ultimately falter. The degree to which resources are utilized to support the organization will determine its longevity. Bernard recognized the decline occurring at the Academy and sought help before the situation became unmanageable.

One of the critical requirements for successful school turnaround system change is effective leadership. Brenda led the Academy's change process with my support.

I was prepared to assist Brenda by drawing on my change experiences from Rockwell Corporation. I consistently implemented a systems change strategy, managing large-scale strategic organizational change as an internal organizational change agent.

Brenda had significant experience in educational organizational change, having served as the head of two private independent schools in the Los Angeles area. While her experiences were similar to mine, they differed in context. However, there are universal change principles necessary for success, regardless of an organization's size, structure, or complexity.

We understood that every organization is unique and requires both similar and distinct change strategies to be effective.

CHAPTER XIV
EFFECTIVE TEACHERS FOR STUDENT LEARNING

Our research on effective teachers in urban schools, like the Academy, indicated that there are three characteristics most directly related to teacher effectiveness at the Academy.

These characteristics are

- *Self-awareness (intrapersonal skills),*
- *Understanding the environment in which they teach,*
- *Maintaining high expectations.*

When we interviewed the teachers upon our arrival at the Academy, we focused on these key characteristics. Specifically, we assessed their seriousness about developing their teaching profession and their commitment to an African-centered philosophy. We were not interested in responses such as, "I teach because it's a convenient job with holidays and summers off," or "because I like children." Surprisingly, we did hear such responses. Instead, we prioritized whether they were team players and if they genuinely believed that all students given the proper opportunity could learn.

In addition, we believed that effective teachers should possess the following qualities:

- **Self-awareness and self-reflection:** Teachers must develop strong intrapersonal skills, understanding their own levels of frustration and coping capabilities (Weiner, 2000).
- **Awareness of their beliefs regarding the capabilities of the Academy's children:** Teachers should recognize how their personal values influence their perceptions, which ultimately affect their expectations and practices (Diffily & Perkins, 2002). In other words, teachers should reflect on their own belief systems and assumptions, particularly when their social backgrounds and experiences differ significantly from those of the students they teach (Weiner, 1993; 1999).

This is why we preferred to hire African American teachers. However, we also hired Teach for America teachers due to their high level of commitment to teaching.

We emphasized that teaching is more than just a job with pay and time off during holidays and summers. Teaching is a noble profession that requires educators to be their best, sharing knowledge and skills with their students. We encouraged the staff to continuously learn, grow, improve, and strive for excellence in their profession, as this directly impacts student learning. After all, isn't that the ultimate goal?

The teachers at the Academy supported the students by creating a welcoming environment. Students would walk in each day and see African words on the walls, books by African American authors on the shelves, and posters of notable African American scholars. They were surrounded by images that reflected their identity. We also introduced the practice of teachers and staff members greeting students and parents at the front door each morning.

Teachers, staff, and students would often wear Dashikis.

A dashiki is a loose-fitting, pullover shirt typically made from vibrant, African-inspired fabric prints. It often features a patch pocket and embroidery at the cuffs and neckline. The dashiki gained popularity in American fashion during the 1960s, embraced by both the Black Pride and white counterculture movements. It became a staple in American ethnic fashion catalogs and, along with other Afrocentric clothing lines, grew in popularity.

Teachers, as well as Brenda and I were referred to as "Mama" or "Baba"—African terms for mother and father—rather than Mr. or Mrs./Miss. However, what truly made this an African-centered Academy was the opportunity given to teachers to be more than just educators. They were encouraged to let the students see them as individuals they could identify with. Teachers got to know the African American students and their families. Any teacher can do that, but at the Academy, this practice was both expected and emphasized.

Effective teachers maintain high expectations for all students, regardless of their backgrounds or where they come from and believe all students can learn.

More important than the curriculum is the question of the methods of teaching and the spirit in which the teaching is given. Bertrand Russel.

When students know teachers care and parents know, students will response in a positive way.

We believed in and reinforced the power that teachers have in influencing student learning by maintaining high expectations. Our study of high-performing schools revealed that this is a key characteristic of their success

CHAPTER XV
CHANGE PRINCIPALS. AND CHANGE STRATEGIES

In this chapter, we will explore the change principles and strategies used in the Academy's Systems Turnaround Change Process.

A Systemic Change Approach:

We approached the Academy's turnaround as a system.

- **Know the Academy:**
  We conducted a four-part, system-wide assessment, which included interviews with faculty, staff students, members of the Board of Trustee, and parents, to gain a comprehensive understanding of the Academy.
- **Effective Change Leadership:**
  Brenda provided effective leadership, and leaders at all levels visibly supported the change by actively participating in the process.
- **People-Centric Change:**
  We involved staff in professional development programs, workshops, retreats, experiential training, classroom observations, and one-on-one meetings to enhance teaching effectiveness.
- **Inclusion:**
  We focused on including all staff affected by the change, ensuring they felt heard and understood the personal benefits of the transformation.
- **Clarify the Direction of the Academy:**
  Staff workshops were conducted to establish consensus on the Academy's vision, mission, strategic direction, and goals.
- **State-of-the-Art Educational System:**
  We introduced a new educational system to support the state-required curriculum and enhance student retention of the learning requirements.
- **Staff Skills Assessment:**
  We interviewed and observed staff to assess their skills, attitudes toward students and teaching, their ability to work as a team, and their commitment to being top educators. As a result of these evaluations, some teachers were asked to leave.

- **Staff Training to Increase Skills:**
  Professional development programs were implemented to increase staff skills, particularly training on the new educational system.
- **New Paradigm of Teaching:**
  We emphasized the relentless use of student assessment data to inform instruction and secured a T.E.A.M. Project Grant to support this initiative.
- **Academy's Culture:**
  We reviewed and transformed the school culture, promoting the recognition of every student's potential and maintaining high expectations for student success, with no excuses.
- **New School Design:**
  A team-based school structure was implemented, creating three small schools within the Academy. This design aimed to elicit high motivation, commitment, and performance from faculty, enhancing student motivation to achieve.
- **Family Group of 10 Students:**
  Every teacher and staff member were assigned a group of 10 students to meet with weekly for one hours, fostering innovation and personalizing student engagement.
- **Brain-Based Instruction:**
  We focused on understanding the brain's role in learning, behavior, and creativity. Teachers were trained on how information is processed by students' brains and the effects of chronic stress on learning and emotions.
- **Expectations of Staff:**
  We shared our high expectations for effective teaching and student learning. Some faculty members resigned, citing the demanding expectations.
- **Student and Teacher Motivation:**
  Strategies were implemented to enhance both student motivation to learn and teacher motivation to teach effectively.
- **Compensation/Reward System:**
  We reviewed and adjusted the compensation system, increasing pay for highly effective teachers and compensating staff for attending workshops on Saturdays. Teachers were incentivized for successful teaching through the T.E.A.M. grant.
- **Discipline System:**
  A new "no tolerance" "problem solving" discipline strategy was implemented.
- **Technology Integration:**
  Interactive whiteboards, classroom computers, and iPads were introduced to enhance teaching and learning.
- **Connecting with Students:**
  Strategies were developed to personally connect and bond with students, showing them that staff cares, which in turn increased their openness to learning.
- **Improved Facility:**
  The Academy's facility was enhanced to be an oasis of learning, with regularly waxed and cleaned floors, organized spaces, student work displays, and pictures of African American leaders on the walls. One of the initial projects we supervised involved students painting and decorating their own bathrooms.

The girls took responsibility for decorating the female restrooms, while the boys did the same for the male restrooms. Our theory was that if students had a personal investment in the space, they would be less likely to deface it with graffiti. This theory proved effective, as students took pride in their efforts and maintained the facilities.

- **Quiet Place Waterfall:**
  A waterfall with Koi fish was installed in the atrium, providing a calming effect for students and teachers. A large tank of goldfish was also placed in the entrance hallway.

- **Order in the Academy:**
  Strategies were implemented to maintain orderly student movement in the halls, to and between classes, lunch, recess, and dismissal. Teachers were trained in classroom management systems.

- **Parental Involvement:**
  We emphasized the critical role of parents as their children's first teachers and engaged them through the *Parents Are Teachers Too* (P.A.T.T.) organization, as well as through student performances.

CHAPTER XVI
IMPLEMENTATION WITH INCLUSION OF STAFF

One of our first tasks was to engage the faculty and staff as active agents of change. We communicated the planned changes for the Academy, seeking their understanding, input, and involvement. Our goal was to ensure that they comprehended how these changes would affect them and to encourage their active participation throughout the process. From the first month of our involvement with the Academy, we began introducing change by educating faculty and staff. We involved all 40 members in the process through a variety of strategies, including workshops, retreats, experiential training, and professional development programs.

The Education of Faculty and Staff as Agents of Change

In advancing the turnaround process, we designed faculty professional development programs, retreats, and workshops to empower teachers as agents of change. We believed that by becoming informed, understanding the benefits, and expressing their preferences, teachers would be more likely to support the changes.

The Power of Education for Change

We understood that those involved in the change would be more likely to support it. Through the collaborative process, they would also come to understand us better and embrace our expectations. We made it clear that we were setting a new direction—symbolically raising a flag and stating, "We are heading this way; stay on board with us, or now is the time to step off."

Throughout our tenure at the Academy, we consistently informed the faculty and staff about the changes we intended to implement through educational sessions, ensuring their understanding and encouraging their input.

We both believed in the power of education to drive change and in involving those affected by the change throughout the process. Our respect for education was grounded in the belief that it empowers individuals to navigate life's challenges, make informed decisions, and contribute actively to society by equipping minds with knowledge, skills, and critical thinking abilities.

Two Retreats

Shortly after Brenda became the Head of the Academy, she and I organized two two-day staff retreats—one in June 2009 and another for faculty in August 2009. This practice was something Brenda had brought with her from her previous school. We were clear in our intention to declare who we are and what we stand for.

The retreats we designed and implemented were opportunities for the entire faculty and staff to come together in a creative and strategic manner. We held these gatherings in the Academy's auditorium, fostering a collaborative space.

During the two-day retreat in June 2009, we celebrated the successes of the past school year. We also reaffirmed our shared commitment: that every child deserves a quality education, effective teaching, and the belief that every student can learn. Furthermore, we emphasized the importance of adopting a team-based organizational structure and cultivating a new culture that prioritizes and supports both teaching and student learning.

We believed that organizational change is crucial for both schools and businesses. It is vital to ensure that staff are fully engaged with the process and outcomes they help create. By involving staff in the change process—especially when it directly affects them—we sought to provide them with a greater sense of control, increase their commitment to the change, and reduce potential resistance.

Research shows that employee engagement is key to successful change management. To facilitate effective organizational change, it is essential to create a unified vision of how the staff will collaborate to make the change initiative a reality.

The Second Retreat, August 2009

During the two-day staff and faculty retreat in August 2009, we focused on reflecting on the lessons learned from the previous school year. We identified what worked well and what changes were necessary. Additionally, we revisited the Academy's vision and mission and set clear goals for the new school year.

As a faculty and staff group, we discussed the Academy's assessment results, gathering feedback to validate our findings. The consensus indicated a collective readiness to move in a new direction.

Key Areas Covered in the Retreats:

- **Clarification of the Academy's New Direction**: Ensuring that everyone understood and aligned with the new trajectory.
- **Review of the School Vision and Mission**: Clarifying the non-negotiable, Academy-wide goals and establishing a new school culture.
- **Implementation of the Family Group of 10 Design for Students**: Strengthening personal connections through small, focused groups.
- **Three Team-Based School Design Concept**: Structuring the school into teams to enhance collaboration and effectiveness.

- **Personal Connections with Students**: Emphasizing the importance of building strong, meaningful relationships with students.
- **Culture of High Expectations**: Reinforcing the need for all faculty and staff to cultivate a culture of high expectations for student success.
- **Focus on Student Learning and Character Development**: Renewing our commitment to enhancing both academic performance and personal growth.
- **Relentless Use of Data**: Using data-driven decision-making as a foundation for all educational strategies.
- **Review and Revision of Policies**: Updating Academy policies related to student discipline, uniforms, and teacher dress code.
- **No Excuses for Lack of Student Learning**: Establishing a no-excuses mindset toward student achievement.
- **Team-Building Skills Training**: Providing faculty and staff with the skills necessary to work effectively as a cohesive unit.

Throughout the retreats, workshops, and professional development programs, the faculty was always actively involved.

CHAPTER XVII
AN OUTLINE AND DETAILS OF THE NEW EDUCATIONAL SYSTEM

The New Educational System

During the retreats, workshops, and professional development programs, Brenda presented an outline of the new educational system and encouraged faculty to share their understanding and comments. She fostered continued faculty engagement and input as the system evolved. Detailed references and further information will follow. The new System.

- **Infusion of Whole-Brain Teaching Strategies**: Implementing these strategies throughout the school environment and in the classroom.
- **Hiring Teach for America Staff**: Bringing in highly motivated educators through the Teach for America program.
- **Emphasis on Higher-Order Thinking Skills**: Encouraging critical and analytical thinking.
- **Authentic Assessments**: Utilizing assessments that measure real-world application of knowledge.
- **"Five a Day" – Repeat, Repeat, Repeat**: Reinforcing core concepts through daily repetition.
- **Project-Based Learning**: Engaging in hands-on learning experiences (Ford PAS training).
- **Singapore Math**: Introducing Singapore's effective math teaching methodology.
- **Partnership with Wayne State University's Math Corps**: Supporting students through this innovative math program.
- **Columbia University's Lucy Calkins Reading and Writing as a Process**: Implementing research-based literacy instruction.
- **Pattern-Based Writing**: Fostering structured approaches to writing.
- **Reading Workshop**: Focusing on individualized reading instruction.
- **Phonics First**: A multisensory approach to teaching reading, writing, spelling, and listening.
- **Zoo-Phonics**: A multisensory approach to teaching language arts.
- **STEM-Related Science**: Integrating science education that focuses on STEM (Science, Technology, Engineering, Math).
- **Gesell Program**: Assessing students for age-appropriate developmental education.
- **Youth Participatory Action Research (YPAR)**: A collaboration with the University of Michigan School of Education and Psychology.

- **Integration of Technology**: Utilizing whiteboards, computers, iPads, iPods, Kindles, and Study Island in classrooms.
- **Facilities Improvements**: Presenting changes to enhance the school's physical environment.

At the Academy, Brenda applied the knowledge she gained from her experience as the Head of a private independent schools in the Los Angeles, CA area. She focused on incorporating proven educational programs aimed at enhancing teaching quality and increasing student academic performance.

Her overarching goal was to ensure that every student received the best possible education and social experiences. As an academic instructional leader, she worked closely with teachers and staff to improve teaching practices and boost student performance.

One of Brenda's greatest strengths was her ability to stay current with successful trends and practices in education. She consistently kept her faculty informed by conducting professional development workshops throughout the year.

Brenda and I conducted ongoing training sessions for teachers to help them incorporate the new educational system. These workshops were held in addition to the fall retreat, which took place before the school year began, and the June retreat held before summer break. The June retreat focused on reflecting on the successes of the year and involved students, gathering their input and suggestions for the upcoming school year. The fall retreat, on the other hand, concentrated on learning new programs to implement in the new school year. Additionally, we held faculty and staff meetings every Friday.

Details: The Educational System Programs with References

The new educational system was introduced to complement the state-required curriculum while enhancing teacher effectiveness and improving student learning outcomes.

Our intent was to offer every student a comprehensive, cutting-edge educational program. As mentioned earlier, the details of the system are provided with references (see below).

The staff appeared eager to learn the new programs, motivated by the goal of improving student learning. Brenda aimed to provide the Academy's students with the same opportunity to experience the high-quality educational systems she had implemented in private independent schools, where parents typically paid $30,000 to $40,000 annually.

The new academic program at the Academy reflected best practices and a high-quality curriculum.

ENGLISH LANGUAGE ARTS

Reading and Writing as a Process
https://www.google.com/search?client=safari&rls=en&q=what+is+writing+as+a+process&ie=UTF-8&oe=UTF-8

At the Academy, we believed that children learn to read by reading frequently and learn to write by writing regularly. Therefore, we integrated the reading/writing process into our curriculum. This approach encouraged students to write daily, as well as to read and be read to every day.

Readers' Workshop: provides extended time for students to read, reflect, and discuss books daily. The focus is on differentiating or personalizing instruction to meet the diverse learning needs of all students while cultivating a love for reading. The Workshop: is an interdisciplinary writing approach designed to build students' fluency in writing through continuous, repeated exposure to the process of writing.

The Writing Process: (pre-writing, writing, revision, editing, publishing, post-writing) informs all aspects of the students' daily writing, whether it be narrative, transactional, or poetic. Peer and faculty conferencing supports these writing initiatives. Students are introduced to the concepts of writing for specific purposes and audiences. Student writing portfolios are continuously updated. Formal grammar instruction is extended, with an emphasis on sentence structure and variety, paragraphing, parts of speech, and punctuation.

Effective oral Presentation: Speaking and listening in-group discussion occurred daily around current issues.

Six Traits of Writing: To enhance students' writing skills, we introduced Pattern Based Writing, a technique grounded in "The Six Traits of Writing." Developed in the 1980s by researchers and educators, this method offers a reliable framework for structuring writing and instruction.

We identified the need for a more structured approach to support students in developing their writing. By implementing Pattern Based Writing, we have provided them with a solid foundation for effective writing.

Five a Day Quizzes: To review material from the previous lesson, students would receive a daily quiz with five problems covering content from the day before and/or earlier taughtnlessons. As they enter the classroom, they were given five minutes to complete the quiz. Once time was up, the class would begin by discussing the answers to each question. This approach not only reinforced the previous day's content but also allowed the teacher to assess each student's understanding. Additionally, it provided a strong foundation for introducing the day's lesson.

Zoo Phonics: The Zoo-phonics curriculum was grounded in research on phonics instruction and is designed to help students develop a strong awareness of the connection between letters and their corresponding sounds in speech. (Zoo-phonics, n.d.)."

"The Zoo-phonics Multi-sensory Language Arts Program, created by award-winning educators, is a distinctive and engaging curriculum that involves a child's entire body—eyes, mouth, ears, touch, mind, and body—using charming animal letters. This playful and concrete approach makes learning enjoyable and effective *https://zoo-phonics.com.*

Study Island: We also integrated Study Island into our curriculum to strengthen students' understanding of core subjects. Study Island is a web-based program for instruction, practice, assessment, and reporting, built on Michigan's state standards. It delivers rigorous, research-based academic content with proven success for all students.

Handwriting Without Tears: Handwriting Without Tears was introduced in our K–3 program. For kindergarteners, the program emphasizes kinesthetic learning as a foundation for writing. The first and second grades, students continue with kinesthetic activities while beginning pencil-paper tasks. By third grade, the curriculum included cursive instruction.

Singapore Math: Singapore Math was first introduced during the 2009-2010 school year and has since been expanded. The school adopted the Math in Focus program from Houghton Mifflin, known for its strong emphasis on developing conceptual understanding. While it aligns with the NCTM (National Council of Teachers of Mathematics) standards prevalent in the U.S., it differs from the original Singapore series by being tailored to these standards.

Unlike most programs aligned with the NCTM standards, Singapore Math does not attempt to cover every concept each year. Instead, it focuses on fewer topics, teaching them in depth so they do not require constant reteaching. Each semester-level Singapore math textbook builds upon prior knowledge and skills, with students mastering them before moving on to new material.

The program's scope and sequence is advanced and has a significant emphasis on preparing students for success in algebra. As a result, algebraic thinking and expressions are introduced early and reinforced throughout the curriculum.

The approach to math in this program is grounded in a solid understanding of number sense, diverging from traditional methods. It builds a strong foundation in number sense and develops it through place-value-based computational strategies.

Math Corps: The Academy established a partnership with Wayne State University's Math Corps program during the 2009-2010 school year. We fully integrated the Math Corps approach into our curriculum, successfully implementing the program for grades 5 through 8 in the 2010-2011 school year.

As a result of this integration, we observed a significant improvement in students' understanding of the material, higher test scores, and increased confidence in both the subject matter and them.

One day during a math lesson in a 5th-grade classroom, I was observing, a student was working on problems that required adding three columns of numbers. The student called me over to him and said, "Baba Warrington, I have a three-column math problem, but I only have two hands to add.

Can I use one of your hands to help me with the third column?" I was more than happy to assist and found his request quite delightful. The smile on his face made it clear that our mission was accomplished. We both left feeling fulfilled.

Science--Hands on Learning: The science program, kindergarten through eighth grade, was an experiential, hands-on program which involves problem solving and critical thinking. Various activities, such as watching the life cycle of a butterfly or tracking hurricanes, provide topics for scientific observation. Students wrote their findings, first in journals and, by middle school, in formal lab reports.

We utilized the online science program *Aha! Science through" Learning.com."* The Aha! Science program integrates the scientific process into instruction by engaging students through interactive games, and inquiry-based activities. This comprehensive program lays the foundation for students to become successful in science, making them comfortable with identifying questions and discovering the process to explore and answer them.

We found this program to be more effective than traditional textbooks because it allowed us to stay updated with the latest research and information. Textbooks quickly became outdated; for example, Pluto was reclassified and no longer considered a planet, altering the number of recognized planets in our solar system, yet the recently purchased textbook still contained outdated information.

STEM (Science, Technology, Engineering, Math): Additionally, we integrated STEM

(Science, Technology, Engineering, Math) through project-based, hands-on learning. This approach incorporates the teaching of subjects like mathematics and science by embedding technology and engineering into the curriculum. STEM is an umbrella term that groups these distinct but interconnected disciplines.

We believe that all students benefit from the STEM hands-on learning program because it fosters independent innovation and allows students to delve deeper into all subjects by applying the skills they learn. These skills are essential for today's students to become tomorrow's global leaders.

Project-Based Integrated Lessons: An example of a project-based integrated lesson that Brenda introduced to the teachers and staff was the weaving of South Carolina baskets using sweetgrass from the Lowcountry of South Carolina.

The integrated lesson included teaching history, reading and writing, math, science, and art. We invited a basket-weaving artist from South Carolina to instruct the teachers in the craft of basket weaving during a faculty and staff retreat.

This basket-making tradition was brought to South Carolina in the 17th century by West African slaves who were brought to America to work on plantations. The climate and landscape of West Africa closely resemble those of South Carolina, where rice had long been cultivated. This craft, passed down through generations since the 1700s, is unique to the Lowcountry and represents one of the oldest West African art forms in America. These beautifully crafted baskets are a cherished Lowcountry tradition—an American art form with African origins. When West African slaves were brought to South Carolina, they carried with them the tradition of weaving baskets from grass, a skill that has endured through the centuries.

Gesell Theory: *https://www.gesell-yale.org/pages/gesell-theory*

The Gesell Institute trained our teachers on how to provide instruction that was developmentally appropriate for each students. Gesell's theory, known as the maturational-developmental theory, serves as the foundation for nearly every other theory of human development.

In the early 20th century, Dr. Gesell observed and documented the patterns of child development, demonstrating that all children progress through similar and predictable sequences, though each child advances at his/her own unique pace.

Dr. Gesell was the first theorist to systematically study developmental stages and to show that a child's developmental age (or stage of development) may differ from their chronological age.

This developmental process is shaped by both internal and external factors. Internal factors include genetics, temperament, personality, learning styles, and physical and mental growth. At the same time, external influences such as environment, family background, parenting styles, cultural factors, health conditions, and early experiences with peers and adults also play a crucial role.

Solution Based Problem Solving: Solution-focused problem-solving concentrates on promoting solutions, rather than searching for causation. This helps to avoid getting caught up in the "blame game," where everyone is blaming rather than problem solving. Students were encouraged to write out the problem and the solution as they saw it. *https://www.google.com/search?client=safari&rls=en &q=solution+focused+problem+solving++in+schools&ie=UTF-8&oe=UTF-8*

Social Studies: Teaching social studies at the Academy is a rich experience. Teachers provide study skills instruction and opportunities to think critically about the patterns in history and current issues in our world. Students participates in mock trials, debates, election returns, and critical-thinking projects.

Social studies allow students to reflect on ways to improve our world and the importance of asking questions. The Academy enables teachers and students to cultivate critical thinkers through their social studies program.

Technology: For technology we adopted the Easy Tech online program through *Learning. Com.* It is a K-8 technology literacy curriculum that integrates technology, 21st century skills, and professional development into core instruction. Easy Tech helps students learn the software program necessary for being prepared for the 21st century and teachers learn how to teach 21st century standards.

Computer Programming/ Coding: We introduced the students to computer coding. Coding allows programmers/students to build programs, such as websites and apps. Computer programmers can also tell computers how to process data in better, faster ways. A programming language/code is a system of notation for writing computer programs.

Interactive White Boards: Interactive whiteboards are classroom tools that allow teachers to display images onto an electronic screen from a computer using a projector. With an interactive whiteboard, teachers can present images, presentations, and videos to the entire class simultaneously. *https://www.google.com/search?client=safari&rls=en&q=white+board+used+in+schools&ie= UTF-8&oe=UTF-8*

Computer Lab: The Academy designated a space in the library equipped with computers and the necessary software to facilitate computer-based learning. Teachers often used this room in conducting lessons on the computers. Additionally, the computers were used for students to take state assessments.

Computers in the Classroom: The grant the Academy received through the T.E.A.M. Project enabled the purchase of a classroom set of computers for students. Brenda implemented a system for students and teachers to sign out the computers.

I Pads in the Classrooms: At Bernard's insistence, we purchased iPads for each high school student for study purposes. Before classes started, Brenda conducted literacy sessions using the I Pads. I sat in on the sessions and was pleased to see the students excitement and interest in reading and discussing books. it.

Go Observe Software: Go Observe Software was a tool Brenda used to conduct faculty evaluations, and teachers used it to write up student observations. This software made it easier to document student records and provide feedback almost immediately. Every Wednesday and Friday, we met with a team of teachers after school to discuss their observations of students and to reflect on what was required to be more effective, what was working, and what needed to be modified. We also sometimes met with teachers during their planning periods. A special focus was placed on discussing the teaching strategies needed to enhance student learning, as well as reviewing Brenda's evaluations of them.

Foreign Language: We introduced Mandarin as the language program for all grades, a program that Bernard was particularly eager to implement. Students learned basic Mandarin vocabulary, such as numbers, colors, days of the week, animals, parts of the body, clothing, and more. Cultural celebrations also enriched the study of Mandarin. The Mandarin program utilized teacher-directed lessons and lectures, Total Physical Response (TPR), small group and pair work, show and tell, and reinforcement games.

The methodologies used include students with a variety of learning styles. Throughout the program, a great emphasis was placed on critical thinking, cultural understanding, and geography, as well as on fundamental skills.

In middle school the Mandarin program's goal included having students attain a measurable degree of communicative competency in Chinese, helping them grow in cultural understanding and awareness, and developing in them an appreciation of the value of learning a second language. Students took written tests and quizzes.

One of the strengths of the program was that students did not just learn language, but they also learn about the regions and peoples who speak the language.

The middle school students, unfamiliar with Chinese people, thought I was Chinese and believed the Mandarin teacher was my daughter. Even the parents shared this misconception. They would often walk into the Academy asking for "the Chinese man."

Fine Arts: At the Academy, we sought to develop the students' skills in the visual arts by using a variety of techniques, tools, and media to formulate their ideas visually, and we put emphasis on teaching them to decode the art of others in our own culture as well as in cultures from other places and times.

Students were also introduced to Art History, with a special emphasis on African Art Forms—an area often overlooked in public schools, where the focus tends to be primarily on European art.

The Academy implemented a drawing program, a music curriculum which was based on singing, chanting rhymes, and playing instruments. Students create, explore, and move while learning the fundamentals of music. In grade school, the student's learned to play the recorder. In the middle school, students were exposed to playing instruments, African drums, trombone, clarinet, trumpet, etc.

We Formed Partnerships --Math Corps: We formed a partnership with Wayne State University's Math Corps program in 2009-2010. We fully integrated the Math Corps approach into our educational system and curriculum, successfully implementing the program for grades 5-8 during the 2010-2011 school year.

As a result of this integration, we saw a marked improvement in students' ability to grasp the material, increased test scores, and enhanced confidence in both the subject matter and them. Brenda and I met weekly with the Math Corps representative from Wayne State University and the Academy's math teachers to discuss student achievements and identify the support needed.

Partnered With the Renaissance Unity Church: We had the opportunity to partner with Renaissance Unity Church in Warren, Michigan, through a project called T.R.U.E. (Timbuktu-Renaissance Unity Education). Members of the church volunteered their time to help the Academy provide a quality education for each of our students.

This collaboration with Renaissance Unity Church was more than just volunteers tutoring children in need. It carried a deeper message by uniting an urban school in Detroit with a suburban church whose core value is service to the community. The Academy's African Drum group even performed at the church on several Sundays, much to the congregation's delight.

The church volunteers attended an orientation during the week of April 26, 2010. During this session, we discussed the Academy's mission and philosophy, what it means to be African-centered, the standards of behavior expected from the volunteers, and their responsibilities. We also gave them a tour of the school and shared best practices for tutoring our students. Six volunteers consistently attended and contributed to the program.

Family Groups: Family Groups were multi-age groups of students that met regularly and remained together throughout their time at the Academy. There were 18 family groups, each including students from kindergarten through eighth grade, with one or two faculty or staff advisors. The older students served as leaders, responsible for planning and guiding the group's activities.

These Family Groups fostered a sense of community while promoting leadership skills and responsibility in the older students. The group activities enriched the school experience by encouraging mutual respect, trust, and support across grade levels. Through this shared experience, students, faculty, and staff became better acquainted with one another.

Whole Brain Teaching: We introduced Whole Brain Teaching, an instructional approach that employs strategies designed to fully engage students' brains, thereby maximizing their involvement in the learning process. By integrating principles of social-emotional learning and neuroscience, this approach transforms the classroom into a dynamic and highly energetic learning environment.

Whole brain learning is a model where learners engage both hemispheres of the brain, rather than relying solely on the left or right side, to grasp concepts more comprehensively.

Whole Brain Teachers of America is a grassroots education reform movement that began in 1999, founded by three Southern California teachers: Chris Biffle, Jay Vanderfin, and Chris Rekstad.

Dr. Kenneth Wesson --Brain-Considerate Learning:

Dr. Kenneth Wesson believes that understanding how the brain works and learns can make one a better teacher." He contends, *"If It's Your Job to Develop the Mind, Shouldn't You Know How the Brain Works?" https://www.cta.org/educator/posts/kenneth-wesson-the-science-of-learning*

Brain-Based: Brain-Based considered learning is a paradigm of learning which addresses student learning and learning outcomes from the point of view of the human brain. It involves specific strategies for learning which are designed based on how human attention, memory, motivation, and conceptual knowledge acquisition

work. *cognitiontoday.com › brain-based-learning-theory-strategies-and-concepts.* In addition, we taught staff whole brain teaching.

Teach Like a champion: We also introduced techniques adopted from Doug Lemov, *Teach Like a champion*

https://www.google.com/search?client=safari&rls=en&q=tetea+like+a+champion&ie=UTF-8&oe=UTF-8

The techniques from *Teach Like a Champion,* included but were not limited to,

1. Setting High Academic Expectations.
2. Planning that Ensures Academic Achievement.
3. Structuring and Delivering a Lesson.
4. Engaging Students in the Lesson.
5. Creating a Strong Classroom Culture.
6. Building and Maintaining High Behavioral Expectations.

7. Building Character and Trust.
8. Supported parent involvement in the Academy, assisting to form a parent organization Parents Are Teachers Too (PATT).

Data-Driven Decision-Making: This system was introduced to the staff through training, as a top priority, in using student data to inform instruction.

With data-driven decision making the teachers gained greater control over the direction of their curriculum and the quality of the student learning. This is because it is based on objective data, concrete evidence and results can be effectively measured to assess impact.

Financial and Health Advice: We offered workshops for staff on financial planning, including investing in an IRA for retirement, as well as sessions on nutrition for health and meditation for stress management. All faculty and staff were given the opportunity to invest in their retirement. *Recently, we spoke with a faculty member who is now benefiting from these investments while raising two children.*

In addition to focusing on teachers' health and financial well-being and implementing the New Educational System to enhance student learning, we continuously sought ways to improve teaching effectiveness. This led us to introduce a new teaching paradigm.

We trained the staff on the brain's role in student learning and the effects of prolonged chronic stress on students' brains, learning, and behavior. Understanding that the brain is the foundation of all learning, we believed it was crucial for teachers to gain a deeper understanding of how the brain influences student learning.

CHAPTER XVIII
THE BRAIN, THE SEAT OF ALL LEARNING A NEW PARADIGM OF TEACHING

As part of the New Educational System we introduced, we placed significant emphasis on understanding the brain's role in teaching, student behavior, and learning. Faculty members were trained on this critical topic to enhance their ability to support students effectively.

- The brain, weighing approximately three pounds and resembling a cauliflower, is a highly complex organ with over a billion cells. It governs thought, memory, emotions, motor skills, sensory processing, vision, breathing, temperature regulation, hunger, and other essential bodily processes.
- Along with the spinal cord, the brain forms the central nervous system (CNS). A key concept for educators is that the brain learns through the senses. One of its remarkable features is neuroplasticity—the ability to continue learning and adapting throughout life.
- The five basic human senses—touch, sight, hearing, smell, and taste—are vital for learning. Sensory organs send data to the brain, enabling students to process and understand their environment.

Understanding the brain is essential for creating effective learning experiences.

According to Daniel G. Amen, M.D., in *Making a Good Brain Great*, *"The brain is the most complicated organ in the body."*

Brain-based learning is an educational approach that examines student learning through how the human brain functions. It involves strategies aligned with human attention, memory, motivation, and knowledge acquisition. We also educated the staff on how prolonged stress impacts students' brains, affecting both learning and behavior (Parker and Parker, *The Brain in School and at Work*, 2009, 2011, in Appendix D.

When introducing the Brain-Based Teaching approach, we conducted workshops centered on the article "The Brain in School and Work" (*Parker and Parker, The Brain in School and at Work*, 2009, 2011, in Appendix D). We asked teachers to read the article and complete a questionnaire before the workshop. During the workshop, we reviewed and discussed their responses.

We were surprised, though perhaps we shouldn't have been, when we asked teachers where the information, they want students to learn is processed. Many were unaware that it enters the brain through the senses. I wasn't certain of this myself until I studied the brain's role in learning. Another question we posed was, if students lack background knowledge before learning a new lesson, what teaching strategies could help them? Again, many were unsure.

We discussed that making the subject matter an emotionally significant event could capture students' attention. Teachers could dramatize the lesson, present it as a story, dress in a way that draws students in, play a game, or find ways to make the content resonate on a personal level.

Know About the Effects of Toxic Stress

We also informed the staff during workshops that another goal of the Academy was to establish a foundation for training teachers on how to counter the effects of chronic stress on students' brains and learning. We shared an article we authored, titled "Chronic Stress and Its Effects on Students' Brains," which is included in the *Appendix E*.

In our article, we highlighted that students living under prolonged stress or experiencing chronic stressors can suffer negative effects on the development of three critical areas of the brain: the prefrontal cortex, hippocampus, and amygdala. These impacts can affect emotional and social regulation, behavior, attention, short- and long-term memory, cognitive development, planning, decision-making, and goal setting. See more information in *Appendix E*.

We provided faculty with research-based teaching strategies to support students living under these conditions, such as acting as a role model of supportive behavior and demonstrating love and care for them.

Further we conducted an Experiential Brain Education Workshop for staff.

The Experiential Brain Education Workshop

In our experience, experiential learning can be particularly powerful for adults, as we have the life experience and cognitive ability to reflect, develop new ideas, and take positive action. It also provides the real-world context needed to apply new skills effectively and to generate new ideas for implementation

An Experiential A two-day training session on Brain Education was conducted to enhance staff knowledge about the brain and its role in student learning. To improve teaching effectiveness, we implemented an experiential, active professional development session focused on Brain Education. We introduced Brain Education activities for teachers to use in their classrooms with students. Bernard attended the training, but the principal at that time refused to participate. We collaborated with the Brain Education Organization from Sedona, AZ.

Brain Education is **a *comprehensive mind-body training system designed to enhance students' physical, emotional, and mental health by developing the brain's capacity*.**

Created in 1980 in South Korea by the author Ilchi Lee, it has been practiced by millions worldwide since its inception. This innovative educational system teaches the true value of the brain and humanity.

We were trained in this methodology and helped train the staff at the Academy. Additionally, we assisted in training educators across the United States to implement this system with their students.

The brain-related activities taught to staff and practiced in their classrooms were intended to increase students' self-confidence and self-esteem. These activities also provided students with tools to recognize, embrace, and harness their inner power to regulate their social and emotional behavior.

During staff training, we provided specific instruction in brain research and curriculum components that incorporate multi-sensory teaching strategies. We also explained a key property of the brain: neuroplasticity, the brain's ability to learn and adapt throughout a lifetime. Neuroplasticity refers to the brain's capacity to form new neurons when students genuinely learn something new from a teacher.

We emphasized that without regular use, newly acquired information can be lost. Therefore, repetition is a critical teaching strategy—it helps students retain new information, along with ensuring they get a good night's sleep.

A Brain Education module was taught every morning for 15 minutes in classrooms. There were indications that students enjoyed the sessions, learning to control their emotions and improve their attention in class.

For some students, their interest in attending school significantly increased. They found Brain Education to be fun and looked forward to the sessions. Students also learned strategies to better manage stress and used guided imagery before spelling tests.

There were also learning opportunities for teachers. Some teachers gained an understanding of the brain's structure and functioning and its critical role in student learning. However, maintaining the Brain Education sessions proved challenging for some, even after we returned twice to reinforce the teaching. To address this, we implemented a research design.

Research Design: *Control Group and an Experimental Group*

In November 2006, the Strengths, and Difficulties (SDQ) standardized questionnaire was completed by teachers for a random sample of fourth-grade students at the Academy and for fourth-grade students in a control group from a neighboring school. In May 2007, the teachers re-administered the SDQ for the same students.

The results indicated a significant improvement in the Academy students in areas such as emotional symptoms, conduct problems, hyperactivity, peer problems, and pro-social behavior. In contrast, the control group students showed no improvement or worsened in all domains except emotional symptoms.

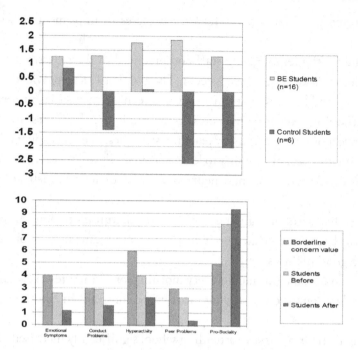

Change in Strength and Difficulties (SDQ) among 4th grade students attending either BE or Control School (Positive value indicates improvement).

We also wanted the teachers and staff to understand that neuroplasticity refers to the physiological changes in the brain that occur because of students learning new information and interacting with their environment.

From the time the brain begins to develop in utero until the day we die, the connections among the cells in our brains help us reorganize in response to changing needs. This dynamic process allows us to learn from and adapt to different experiences throughout our lifetime. — Celeste Campbell (n.d.).

We also addressed the detrimental impact of angry yelling and dismissing students on their brain development, which we observed during our assessment visit to the Academy. Some teachers exhibited this behavior, and we emphasized the need for change. While training educators in the new educational system and brain-based learning is crucial, it is equally important for teachers to be effective instructors who ensure their students are mastering the material.

As mentioned earlier, we introduced teachers to the effects of long-term chronic stress on students' brains.

A variety of life experiences can cause severe stress in children, often starting in early childhood. When children experience traumatic events, it can lead to the development of chronic stress that may persist into adulthood.

Examples of conditions that may cause chronic stress in children include:

- Mental illness in one or more parents
- Emotional, physical, or sexual abuse
- Substance misuse in the family

- Parental divorce
- Homelessness
- Prolonged fear of gang violence
- Fear of physical harm
- Witnessing the murder of a parent, sibling, relative, or friend
- Incarceration of a parent or close family member

We knew that some of the Academy's students were living under these types of conditions. We wanted the teachers to understand the importance of always being a positive role model, connecting with students, repeating lessons, offering compliments, and reinforcing their care for the students.

We also conducted a teacher workshop on our article "The Brain at School and Work." *Appendix D.* We asked staff to answer a questionnaire we developed based on the article before the workshop and then read our article. We discussed the correct answers in the workshop and had a lively give and take discussion.

We indicated in our article, that students living under prolong stress, experiencing chronic stressors can have a negative effect on the development of three parts of a child's brain: the prefrontal cortex, hippocampus, and amygdala.

The prefrontal cortex is an important part of student's brains. It is at the front of the frontal lobe, which is immediately behind the forehead. It affects students' behavior, personality, and ability to plan.

Students' hippocampus is a small part of your brain with a big job; it helps with their learning and memory. It converts short-term memories into long-term memories by organizing, storing, and retrieving memories within your brain.

Our research indicated the prolonged stress conditions student live under can hijack the amygdala, which controls the fight or flight behavior. Many students stay in a fight mode. When we first started to manage the Academy, we observed four-five fights, a day. We wondered why and conducted research on the brain and behavior, and we got a hint. Living under toxic stress conditions, by writing the chronic stress article in the appendix.

We embarked on a path to design and conduct ongoing professional development and write research articles shared with staff that would:

We embarked on a mission to design and conduct ongoing professional development and to write research articles to share with staff that would:

- Expose and enlighten every staff and faculty member to brain education research and its implications for student learning.
- Teach faculty, staff, parents, and students learning approaches that align with how the brain learns best.
- Share research regarding the impact of poverty on the brain as a stressor and offer indicators to identify these effects in students' behavior and achievement.
- Prevent the over-identification of students who perform poorly academically and behaviorally as having a special education disability.
- Train staff to use a multi-sensory approach to instruction that engages multiple senses and pathways of learning (visual, auditory, kinesthetic, etc.).

- Train faculty and staff in effective teaching strategies that engage students in activities designed to maximize the brain's neuroplasticity and restore brain function that may have been negatively affected by chronic stress due to poverty.
- Train faculty in Whole Brain Teaching strategies, where methods are aligned with cognitive science and emphasize the need for extensive practice to achieve mastery in learning.
- Teach staff the Ten-Minute Rule of Student Attention and the importance of incorporating movement to enhance learning. The ten-minute rule is that your audience/students will checkout after ten minutes if there is no change in what you are doing or saying. *Brain Rules 12 principles for Surviving and Thriving at Work, Home, and School, John Medina, 2008.* This means that you need to work to grab your audience's attention repeatedly.

In addition to our workshops on the brain and learning we invited Dr. Wesson to conduct a workshop for the staff on Brain-Considerate Learning. He contends that "If It's a teachers Job to Develop the Mind, Shouldn't they Know How the Brain Works?" ***https://www.cta.org/educator/posts/kenneth-wesson-the-science-of-learning***

His approach involves specific strategies for learning which are designed based on how human attention, memory, motivation, and conceptual knowledge acquisition work. cognitiontoday.com › brain-based-learning-theory-strategies-and-concepts.

In addition, we taught staff whole brain teaching which we covered previously.

Whole Brain Teaching

https://wholebrainteaching.com/about-us/.
Whole Brain Teachers of America is a grass roots, education reform movement begun in 1999 by three Southern California teachers: Chris Biffle, Jay Vanderfin, and Chris Rekstad. Since then, they have been joined by a dedicated group of K-12 educators who form their Executive Board.

Whole Brain Teaching addressed both academics and behavior and how to make teaching FUN. It is One of the best Self Managing class techniques, we have ever seen!

Whole brain teaching is an instructional approach that is the integration of social-emotional learning into a highly energetic, authentically engaged learning process. There is a basic lesson structure that each learning moment follows, giving students ownership of their learning through mimicry. www.teachhub.com › professional development › 2017. cognitiontoday.com › brain-based-learning-theory-strategies-and-concepts.

Whole Child Centered Learning: Whole child-centered learning is the idea that children learn best when all their needs are met social-emotional, physical, mental, intellectual, and need for relationships. Brenda would remind teachers "when children know you care, they will listen to you." Brenda would often say, it is important to take care of student's social needs, it will help them to be open to learn.

In addition to introducing the new powerful Educational System, and information about the brain and student learning. We informed the faculty and staff in a workshop that we were organizing the Academy in a Team-Based System.

CHAPTER XIX
THE TEAM-BASED STRUCTURE

Based on my experiences as an internal organizational change agent in the Rockwell Corporation, and Brenda's experience as head of a private, independent school, we focused on changing the school's design to a team-based system. The new design was intended to elicit high performance, high motivation, and high commitment from the staff, while improving student academic achievement. Dr. R. Walton, Harvard Business School, a friend, "From Control to Commitment."

Team Based Structure Important in Business

In my experience working at Rockwell, I found that teamwork is one of the most crucial tools for organizational efficiency and for addressing the socio-psychological needs of employees. While we all agree that teamwork is important, not everyone fully appreciates its impact in the workplace. Teamwork in the workplace involves a group of individuals working together efficiently toward a collective goal.

When multiple people collaborate toward a common objective, the organization can thrive. We believed that fostering teamwork in the Academy would lead to more effective teaching and enhanced student learning, with a focus on ensuring that students master the Grade Level Content Expectations (GLC). GLCs describe what students are expected to know to be successful at any given grade level.

The team structure at the academy was designed to support the new Educational System and the other changes we were implementing, with active staff involvement. This team-based organization required teachers to collaborate for the benefit of student learning. To successfully implement this system, it was essential to teach the staff the team-building social skills necessary for effective teamwork.

Team Based System African Centered Style

Working in Teams

Working in teams and fostering teamwork can help build strong relationships between teachers, students, and parents. This collaborative environment can enhance students' desire to succeed academically, socially, and emotionally, helping them to develop their Nia (purpose) in life.

Umoja Teams Concept

7 Principles and Ma'at (pronounced may-et), Concept

We organized the Academy into an Umoja Team-based structure, consisting of three small, personalized schools within a school, with each team of teachers responsible for a specific school division (K–2, 3–5, 6–8). Umoja Teams (Umoja means unity) are analogous to "Professional Learning Communities" (DuFour and DuFour). Each team was responsible for each student for three years.

The Seven Principles

The Academy based its philosophy on the ancient Egyptian concept of Ma'at and the principles and values of Nguzo Saba, a Swahili term meaning Seven Principles. These principles and values were integral to the Team-Based organization.

Ma'at (pronounced may-et) is the ancient Egyptian goddess of truth, justice, harmony, and balance—a concept known as Ma'at in Egyptian culture. This idea first emerged during the period known as the Old Kingdom (c. 2613–2181 BCE), though it likely existed in some form earlier.

The Seven Nguzo Principles:

- *Unity*
- *Self-determination*
- *Collective work and responsibility*
- *Cooperative economics*
- *Purpose*
- *Creativity*
- *Faith*

These principles were embedded within the teams throughout the school.

Umoja (Unity Teams)

The Academy's Team-Based structure consisted of three small, personalized schools within a school, known as Umoja (Unity Teams), which practiced synergistic methods to enhance student motivation and staff commitment. A key focus of the system was to increase opportunities for personalized attention for each student.

Synergistic Teams

African culture has long understood the concept of synergy, and the Umoja Teams symbolize synergistic practices. In this context, synergy is defined as "not my way, not your way, but a third way that is better than either of us could achieve individually." The primary focus of Umoja Teams is student learning. The teams are dedicated to the work of schools—student learning and teaching.

Synergistic [Umoja] teams capitalize on individual strengths so that the whole becomes greater than the sum of its parts. According to Stephen R. Covey in The 7 Habits of Highly Effective People, synergy is "the fruit of mutual respect—of understanding and even celebrating one another's differences in solving problems and seizing opportunities."

This approach has been practiced by African people for millennia. Furthermore, as Umoja Team members interact with each other, work with students, and engage with parents, they create a synergistic, personalized school community—a student-centered village, a school family—reflecting what is inherent in African cultural heritage. It takes a community (a village) to raise children.

K–2 Umoja Team

All teachers responsible for grades K–2 function as a team, collaboratively working to ensure the success of all students in these grades over a three-year period. The team members work together to achieve results greater than the sum of their individual efforts for the benefit of student learning and achievement.

Each team followed a consistent format, as demonstrated by the K-2 team. For example, at the start of the school year, the kindergarten teacher would meet with the first-grade teacher to discuss the academic and social/emotional background of students transitioning from kindergarten to first grade. Throughout the year, teachers collaborated to improve the curriculum based on student performance and ensure alignment with the Michigan Grade Level Expectations (GLC).

3–5 Umoja Team

Similarly, all teachers assigned to grades 3–5 operate as a team, following the format as K-2 and collaborating to ensure the success of all students in these grades over three years.

6–8 Umoja Team

The same structure applies to all teachers responsible for grades 6–8. Teachers work as a team, following the format as K-2 and collaboratively striving for the success of all students over three years.

Each team functions as a small school within a school, with the responsibility and accountability for setting a vision, achieving it, and setting goals and objectives for student learning within the context of the overall school goals.

Leadership

Leadership within the teams was rotated monthly. The team leader's primary goal was to lead the team in significantly improving student learning and achievement, enhancing students' social and emotional development, and the students scoring above the norm on required state standardized assessments. Team leaders were also involved in interviewing prospective teachers for the team.

The size of each group of students and teachers varied depending on enrollment in the respective grades.

We also encouraged teachers to team-teach and take turns teaching each other's subjects for variety and learning. For example, Students could be grouped dynamically by knowledge-based acquisition especially in math in grades 3–5. The dynamic grouping was based on Gesell's theory known as a maturational-developmental theory

The teachers could team teach in sharing the division of labor between them to plan, organize, instruct, and make assessments on the same group of students, generally in a common classroom.

In addition to the team-based structure, we also introduced family groups.

As the name suggests, **Family Groups** involve teachers and staff members organizing children of different ages and grade levels into a cohesive unit, like how siblings interact within a family. This approach brings the benefits of family life into the school setting, offering children a broader range of friendships, role models, and opportunities for guidance.

Each teacher and staff member is assigned 10-12 students from various grades, remaining with this multi-grade group for three years, akin to the concept of looping. Some Family Groups had two adult leaders. These teachers met with their Family Group (FG) weekly for approximately one to three hours to teach, tutor, counsel, coach, and create learning experiences tailored to the students' needs. Cooperative learning was emphasized, fostering a sense of responsibility for one another, much like a family, as they worked together to achieve their goals. This structure allowed teachers and staff members to develop a deep understanding of the students and build strong relationships with their parents or guardians.

Professional Learning Communities

(DuFour and DuFour)

We realized that, despite all our efforts to assist students in learning, their motivation to learn is crucial, as is the need for motivated instructors. Professional Learning Communities (PLCs) are an ongoing process where educators work collaboratively in teams, engaging in recurring cycles of collective inquiry and action research to achieve better outcomes for the students they serve. PLCs operate on the belief that continuous, job-embedded learning for educators is key to improving student learning.

(The reference to the link "*www.theprincipalsplaybook.com*

'instructional-leadership › Dufour" has been omitted, as it's generally not included in narrative text.

There are numerous books and videos that promote the idea that the most effective strategy for helping all students achieve high levels of learning is to develop their capacity to function as a professional learning community.

We also recognized that, despite all the efforts to assist students in learning, they must be motivated to learn, and this requires motivated instructors.

CHAPTER XX
STUDENT MOTIVATION TO LEARN

Student motivation has a powerful influence on learning outcomes, with research indicating that unmotivated students are at a higher risk of dropping out. Engaged and driven students are more likely to succeed, so educators should take proactive steps to help students find and maintain their motivation.

The following actions are known to enhance student motivation to learn:

- Establish strong, personalized connections with students.
- Involve students in their learning by encouraging them to take an active role.
- Show genuine care and love for students.
- Use tough love when necessary.
- Set high but achievable expectations for each student.
- Provide a safe and secure learning environment.
- Understand each student as an individual.
- Offer opportunities for student leadership and responsibility.
- Allow students to be partners in their learning and give them a voice.
- Incorporate hands-on learning into lessons.
- Use engaging and relevant teaching strategies and activities.
- Recognize that student learning involves social, neural, and behavioral dimensions, and consider these in all teaching strategies.
- Utilize various senses to help students learn and retain lessons.

Student motivation is further enhanced when teachers, peers, parents, and guardians acknowledge and recognize each student's success. A teacher's personal connection with students, combined with recognition of their achievements, can lead to students feeling good about themselves. This combination positively impacts their self-esteem, self-confidence, and motivation to continue learning, eventually fostering an "I can do it" attitude.

When teachers personally connect with students and show interest by providing support and praise, they stimulate the release of serotonin, a neurotransmitter in the student's brain. Serotonin opens students' minds to new ideas and creates a desire to connect with their teachers and support whatever the teachers require.

When students feel good about themselves, another neurotransmitter called endorphins is released into the brain, helping them relax and feel better. The statement about serotonin was made by Ellen Weber, Ph.D., Director of the MITA International Brain-Based Center, in reference to people at work.

However, if teachers yell angrily, verbally put down, berate, or reject students in their interactions at school, it causes physical pain in the brain. This social pain is just as harmful as physical pain, leading students to become demotivated, disruptive in the classroom, disengaged, prone to mistakes, or develop a "don't care" attitude.

Furthermore, when students perceive that they are being treated unfairly by teachers, it diminishes them and triggers the release of cortisol in the brain. This causes the brain to shut down, closing off to new ideas and reducing the student's willingness to learn or comply with the teacher's expectations.

CHAPTER XXI
A MOTIVATED STAFF AND STUDENT LEARNING

We understand how crucial it is to increase students' motivation to learn, and it is equally important to have a highly motivated staff.

A motivated teacher is essential to a successful classroom and effective student learning. A motivated teacher doesn't just transmit information; they ignite a passion for learning that can last a lifetime. When teachers are motivated and connect with students, they see teaching not as a job but as a mission. This enthusiasm is contagious, inspiring students to aim higher and push their boundaries further.

The following key behaviors are known to elicit high commitment, high employee motivation, and high employee performance from staff:

- Involve teachers in decision-making processes; be inclusive.
- Treat teachers with respect and dignity.
- Delegate responsibility and accountability to teachers, allowing them to succeed in their work based on established goals.
- Provide teachers with opportunities to contribute to society.
- Offer autonomy and greater flexibility in performing their work.
- Assign challenging work that stimulates growth.
- Create opportunities for personal growth and development.
- Provide variety in work and teaching routines.
- Encourage the exchange of help and mutual respect among colleagues.
- Ensure that teams and individuals can relate their work to providing value to students and achieving the school's goals (e.g., three years with students).
- Foster a school culture that supports mutual trust and open communication among staff, which is critical to achieving and sustaining an effective, synergistic team-based academy.
- Ensure perceived adequate and fair compensation and a reward system.
- Provide effective supervision.
- Minimize status differences within the staff.
- Involve teachers in decisions that affect their work.
- Support continuous learning and build trust within the staff.

To further enhance teacher motivation, we emphasized training in teamwork skills, ensuring they could work effectively in collaborative settings.

Teamwork Skills for effective team functioning:

- Effective listening and communication skills
- Brainstorming techniques
- Intrapersonal and interpersonal development
- Understanding the difference between process and content in group dynamics
- Problem-solving strategies
- Navigating the dynamics of change
- Providing constructive feedback, particularly when requested
- Managing conflicts and misunderstandings
- Trusting and utilizing intuitive sense
- Consensus decision-making processes

Teachers were also introduced to the concept of group decision-making, highlighting its potential to be more effective than individual decisions. To illustrate this, we incorporated the N.A.S.A group exercise. Additionally, we reviewed the typical stages teams and groups go through to reach productivity.

Tuckman's stages of group development outline the common steps most teams experience during their formation and progression. Originally, Tuckman identified four stages, with a fifth stage added later. These stages are:

1. **Forming**
2. **Storming**
3. **Norming**
4. **Performing**
5. **Adjourning** (or **Mourning**)

Each stage encourages specific individual and team improvements, ultimately leading to the successful completion of a team's project. Participants were expected to use consensus decision-making during and after the sessions.

In retrospect, we should have dedicated more time to training staff in these skills. Additionally, it would have been beneficial to reinforce the primary purpose of the team meetings, which was to discuss the academic status of their students—not to plan birthday parties and field trips.

Brenda and I attended the team meetings at 7:00 AM to remind the team of the meetings' focus. The goal of these meetings was to discuss students' academic progress and identify the teaching strategies needed to enhance that progress.

Beyond the team concept, we recognized the need for a new school culture to support the team structure, the new Educational System, and to foster the motivation of both staff and students. The Academy's assessment results further underscored the necessity of cultivating a school culture that supports effective teaching and student learning.

CHAPTER XXII
NEW SCHOOL CULTURE

The Academy's New Culture

The tenets of the Academy's New Culture provided a model for teachers and staff to support. It was crucial for the faculty and staff to adhere to these principles.

The Tenets Included:

- Safe and orderly classrooms as the norm.
- A "no tolerance policy" for violent behavior, bullying, and misbehavior.
- Students are always approached in a calm, caring, and respectful manner.
- Student character, personal responsibility, accountability, self-discipline, and high moral standards are highly valued.
- A sense of independence and creative self-efficacy is promoted.
- Curiosity and questioning are encouraged.
- The curriculum and teaching strategies promote learning, happiness, health, self-esteem, self-confidence, and inner peace.

I n the new culture, we believed in celebrating a sense of humor, the joy of happiness, and the ability to be happy. A culture that supports faculty conversations about student learning is essential. Happiness is an inner gift that every human being possesses, and it is a daily personal choice and decision.

Happiness is a matter of personal "choice, not chance."

We cannot make students or others happy if we are not happy ourselves. Happiness is an inner state of well-being. At the Academy, we encouraged everyone to demonstrate, reach out, share, and smile. Living the tenets of happiness is possible only NOW, not in the future. While this may seem like a soft approach to educating students, it is highly effective in connecting with them.

We also wrote an article for teachers titled "Happy Teachers, Happy Students.", *Brain World*. (Appendix)

"Happiness -- A daily expectation at the Academy" keep a smile on your face it can make you feel good and have a positive effect on the students.

We can provide support for teachers, but without effective teaching, student learning will decline. Effective teachers must cultivate a positive school culture that supports student learning and stay current with the latest educational research in their profession. They should consistently strive to be the best-trained professionals in teaching.

CHAPTER XXIII
HIGH EXPECTATIONS FOR STUDENT LEARNING

Effective teachers believe they are responsible for teaching students successfully (Brophy, 1999; Zeichner, 2003) and maintain high expectations that all students can learn.

Effective teachers at the Academy were aware of their own personal beliefs and philosophies, understanding that their backgrounds may differ from those of their students. They selected strategies, methods, and materials that engaged their learners, enabled students to relate learning to their lives, and ultimately led to increased achievement.

We also hired teachers from Teach for America for both the elementary and high school levels. These educators related well to the students and constituted an exceptional group of devoted, enthusiastic teachers who connected effectively with the students in the Academy. They were caring and highly effective educators.

Our decision to hire them was driven by Teach for America's mission "to work toward the day when every child will receive an excellent and equitable education." The organization seeks and nurtures leaders who commit to expanding opportunities for low-income students, beginning with at least two years of teaching in a public school.

The individuals we hired from Teach for America were indispensable to our success. They shared our vision and worked hand in hand with us to implement programs and achieve goals aimed at improving student learning. The Teach for America members we hired demonstrated an impressive work ethic. More information can be found at **https://www.teachforamerica.org**

Effective instructors understand that students learn more quickly and retain more information when the subject matter is personally relevant. Engaging in active learning makes it deeply personal. As Sir Richard Branson says, "You don't learn to walk by following rules. You learn by doing, and by falling over." He described this as learning through experience, also known as project-based learning or experiential learning. As discussed earlier, Brenda taught the teachers project-based learning to enhance their teaching effectiveness. We encouraged teachers to implement project-based learning strategies, a form of experiential student learning, in their classrooms.

Research defines experiential learning as "the process of learning through experience" and, more specifically, "learning through reflection on doing." This process involves self-initiative, self-assessment, and hands-on activities, allowing both students and teachers to benefit from the numerous advantages of experiential learning in the classroom.

We recognized that to support teachers in their efforts to be effective, it was crucial to also address student discipline.

CHAPTER XXIV
NO TOLERANCE DISCIPLINE POLICY

We knew from experience that it was essential to assist effective teachers in controlling disruptive student behavior in the classroom and throughout the Academy. One of the primary complaints identified in the Academy's assessment was the lack of consistency in student discipline.

We implemented a "no tolerance" policy for fighting, bullying, and serious behavioral violations in 2009, following the faculty and staff retreat. Initially, this led to an increase in suspensions, but administration and staff stayed the course and observed a relative decrease in the percentage of students suspended during the first two quarters of the 2011–2012 school year.

The No Tolerance strategy included a "plan of action" involving a contract signed by the parent, student, and an administrator or faculty member. This contract outlined the student's action plan and the interventions or support they would receive. Students were also given the option to serve in-school or after-school detention instead of being suspended.

We believed that student behavior in the Academy could be positively influenced by cultivating a culture that supports high expectations for success. There are no excuses for low achievement, only solutions for improvement, which include increased instructional time, more time on task, extended school days and school years with Saturday and summer instruction, the relentless use of data, ongoing diagnostic assessment of student progress, and multiple opportunities for improvement.

As part of the No Tolerance strategy, teachers were encouraged to connect with students, get to know them well, and demonstrate care and belief in their potential. They were also urged to avoid angry yelling, harsh tones, or sarcasm.

When teachers personally connect with and show interest in students by providing support and praise, they stimulate the release of serotonin, a neurotransmitter that opens students' minds to new ideas and creates a desire to engage with teachers. Similarly, when students feel good about themselves, endorphins are released, helping them to relax and feel better. Ellen Weber, Ph.D., Director of the MITA International Brain-Based Center About People at Work, highlighted these effects.

However, if teachers yell angrily, verbally put down students, or reject them, it causes social pain, which is as harmful as physical pain in the brain. This can lead to students becoming demotivated, disruptive, and disengaged in the classroom.

When students perceive unfair treatment by teachers, it can trigger the release of cortisol, leading the brain to shut down, making it difficult for students to be receptive to new ideas or willing to learn.

To support effective teaching, we emphasized the importance of maintaining order in the Academy. We established guidelines for student behavior in hallways, classrooms, during lunch, dismissal, and on field trips. We believed that maintaining order would assist teachers in being more effective in their roles.

CHAPTER XXV
ORDER IN THE ACADEMY

We worked diligently to establish systems and processes to support effective teaching and student learning. Brenda implemented a system for students to walk in an orderly fashion down the halls, avoiding running during transitions and dismissal. To assist with this, the janitorial staff painted lines in the halls to guide students.

Brenda and I also trained teachers in maintaining classroom order and attention. The training aimed to unify the approach teachers took to establish order in their classrooms.

We emphasized to the teaching staff that after preparing their classroom and setting a calm learning environment, the next step was to establish clear expectations and rules. These guidelines help guide students' behavior, providing structure and predictability, which fosters a positive learning environment.

We believed that students and teachers thrive in environments with some structure. This belief was reinforced by findings from the OECD's Program for International Student Assessment *(PISA) 2009 report)*.

The report showed that most students in PISA-participating countries experience orderly school environments, which are strongly related to better student performance.

For example, more than two out of three students across OECD countries reported that noise and disorder are rare in their classrooms. In countries like Korea, Thailand, Japan, Kazakhstan, and Shanghai-China, fewer than one in ten students reported disruptions that hinder learning.

However, orderly classrooms and schools are not ends in themselves; they are preconditions for learning. In the 55 countries and economies that participated in *PISA 2009,* students in schools with a more conducive classroom climate tend to perform better academically. Even when accounting for socio-economic status, a positive disciplinary climate in school can help level the playing field, giving students from all backgrounds an equal chance to succeed.

In more orderly classrooms, students are empowered to seize learning opportunities and work towards realizing their potential. ***PISA: www.oecd.org/pisa/***

PISA in Focus No.32: Do students perform better in schools with orderly classrooms?

We also introduced and established protocols for substitute teachers and a system for student enrollment, assigning a head for each. This had previously caused confusion in the Academy.

Warrington walking down the hall in order with a group of students and experienced:

I was walking down the hall with students in the Academy and a group of students were walking behind me and asked, "Baba Warrington" (Baba is an African term that means father), "Do you know how to make Egg Foo Yung and shrimp fried Chinese rice? I said yes. Would you please teach us how to cook them? Do you know how to eat with chopsticks?" Please teach us.

I was slow to respond, surprised by the questions, because I didn't realize they thought I was Chinese. I was slow on the intake.

To try make sure they understood that I was African American, I jokingly told this group of students that I was once a slave on a plantation in Mobile, Alabama, where I met Mama Brenda, the most beautiful woman on the plantation.

I didn't share this story with Brenda, so she was surprised when the students caught up with her and asked how she met Baba Warrington on a plantation. She looked at me with a surprised expression and asked, "What did you tell these students?

At another time, I was walking down the hall with Brenda, my wife, when several students caught up with us and said, "Baba Warrington, is that your lady?" I responded, "Yes, it is." They then asked, "How long have you been with your lady?" I replied, "A long, long, long time..." The student responded, "Five years, Baba?" I was surprised by their answer. At that time, we had been married for over 50 years. I didn't attempt to explain the full 50 years.

We introduced systems for order in the Academy and classrooms. We also were clear to staff about how important it was to connect with students, and how that can assist students with their behavior and can add to the motivation of students to learn.

CHAPTER XXVI
CONNECTING WITH STUDENTS

An Impact on Students Learning

Students can feel good about themselves in school when others—teachers, peers, and parents/guardians—acknowledge and recognize their successes. A teacher's personal connection with students can significantly boost their self-esteem, self-confidence, and motivation to learn. This combination can ultimately instill an "I can do it" attitude in students.

We shared various strategies focused on building connections with students, and Brenda was exceptional at this. Every morning, we stood at the front door of the Academy, greeting students with warm hugs. If parents accompanied them, they also received a welcoming hug.

Teachers were encouraged to stand at their classroom doors to greet each student with a warm smile. Additionally, we asked teachers to dedicate the first three days of the new school year to getting to know their students well.

Teachers were provided with various techniques, such as personally interviewing each student and having them complete an interest inventory. During these first three days, students were also asked to introduce themselves to the class through get-acquainted exercises. The warm welcoming of students and parents/guardians at the school's front door continued throughout the school year. Brenda and I firmly believed in the power of warm hugs, and this was all before COVID.

Daily Fights Between Students Declined

In our first month at the Academy, we encountered daily fights between students, sometimes even two or three in a single day. Brenda addressed these incidents with a calm, caring, and problem-solving approach. Along with the assistant principal, Mama Cha-Rhonda Edgerson (now Dr. Edgerson), they spent time with each student involved, asking them to write down their perception of the event and what led to the fight.

Students were then asked to reflect on how they could have avoided the fight, and to share their suggested solutions. Often, they provided excellent insights, and each student was given the benefit of the doubt. This process allowed Brenda and the assistant principal to better understand and connect with each student.

This approach helped the administration demonstrate patience, trust, care, and love, helping students recognize their inner power to avoid conflicts by making conscious choices. Avoiding fights became the new norm at the Academy.

If a student was repeatedly involved in fights, they were suspended for a day and could only return with their parent/guardian. This form of tough love was always administered with care, and parents supported the administration, appreciating the focus on their child's success.

As a result of these efforts, we saw angry, tough students respond positively to the care shown toward them. Within six weeks, daily fights, were reduced to about two per week, and many students began coming to the office proudly stating, "I worked to avoid a fight because I am here to learn." Eventually, avoiding conflicts became more common than engaging in them.

The same caring approach was applied to students displaying other disciplinary issues or disrupting classrooms. We found that students with behavior problems often lacked understanding of the material being taught and acted out to cover up their struggles. The principal and assistant principal met with these students, asking them to write about the issue and suggest solutions.

This process showed students that the administration believed in them, cared for them, and was committed to helping them succeed. The approach emphasized the importance of self-regulation and helped students understand that the ability to control behavior and emotions, as well as the motivation to learn, comes from within.

The power of faculty and staff caring, connecting, and bonding with students is supported by several studies. Cruickshank, Jenkins, & Metcalf (2003) note that "good teachers are caring, supportive, concerned about the welfare of students, knowledgeable about their subject matter, able to get along with parents...and genuinely excited about the work that they do...effective teachers are able to help students learn" (p. 329).

The Committee for Children (2010) cited a long-term study by the Social Development Research Group in Seattle, which followed hundreds of students over more than a decade. The study found that improving teaching practices, cooperative learning, and social problem-solving skills led to higher academic achievement, lower delinquency rates, and decreased rates of health-compromising behaviors among children who felt a strong sense of school connectedness.

Other factors associated with school bonding included lower rates of misbehavior, grade repetition, dropping out, and involvement in criminal or gang activity during adolescence. Additionally, school bonding was linked to increased social skills and greater academic achievement, with these effects extending to high-risk groups such as aggressive boys, children with parents who modeled problem behaviors, and low-income students.

Seattle's Social Development Group also examined a prevention intervention in high-risk neighborhoods, which enhanced school bonding by improving teachers' classroom management and engagement strategies. This led to increased school bonding and achievement, along with a decline in problem behaviors, compared to students not in the program. Those who participated had higher levels of school bonding throughout middle and high school, with higher academic achievement and fewer high-risk behaviors in their senior year.

The academic program at the Academy was designed to reflect best practices and a high-quality curriculum. The Academy aimed to offer every student a comprehensive, data-driven educational program that included Common Core State Standards and mastery of the GLCEs. Teachers were asked to regularly analyze student performance data to guide their instruction, long-term planning, and individualized learning plans.

We believed strongly in the connection between instructors, students, and parents, as it creates a better learning environment and positively affects student behavior and attention in the classroom. When students know you care, they are more open to listening.

In addition to emphasizing the importance of connecting with students, we informed teachers that data-driven decision-making can also improve teaching effectiveness and student learning. The staff was eager to learn how to use data to benefit student learning, including developing individualized student plans and sharing them with parents/guardians. Brenda would meet with teachers to review these plans.

Using assessment data to inform instruction was as crucial as connecting with students and parents, training teachers in team skills, and developing a new culture. This included introducing a new educational system and implementing strategies to motivate both teachers and students through the use of data-driven instruction.

CHAPTER XXVII
DATA-DRIVEN DECISION-MAKING (DDDM) PROCESS A PARADIGM SHIFT

Student Assessment Data Focused on Teaching and Student Learning

We believed in implementing a data-driven decision-making (DDDM) process of teaching at the Academy. It would provide better and more thorough information about the strengths and weaknesses of each student, thus providing the instructors with added means of assisting them on an individual basis and in a group in the classroom.

Data-driven decision-making required an important paradigm shift for teachers at the Academy – a shift from day-to-day instruction that emphasizes the process of teaching and delivery in the classroom, to pedagogy that is dedicated to producing a product, student learning. It provides the opportunity for teachers to understand the individual academic needs of students.

Classroom teaching extends beyond merely completing the teaching process or assigning homework. The true measure lies in what students are actually learning from these activities. Educational practices in the classroom should be evaluated based on their direct impact on student learning. We must focus more on the intentional assessment and analysis of student progress to ensure that teaching is effective and adjust as necessary.

We asked the teachers to implement the key elements of the Academy's data-driven instruction process:

- **Collect Baseline Data:** During the first two weeks of the school year, gather comprehensive baseline data in reading, writing, and math for each student. Enter these results into PowerSchool for tracking.
- **Utilize PowerSchool:** PowerSchool provides a unified platform for all classroom, instruction, assessment, and student data needs. It offers an easy-to-use online K-12 gradebook that simplifies grading, tracks student progress, and saves time for teachers.
- **Develop Measurable Instructional Goals:** Based on the assessment results, set clear, measurable instructional goals for each student. Incorporate these goals into each student's Individual Learning Plan (ILP) and involve parents in developing and supporting the learning plan.
- **Create an Individual Learning Plan (ILP):** An ILP is a strategic, personalized blueprint designed to support each student's unique learning journey. It captures the learner's educational and developmental needs, including their goals, learning preferences, strengths, and interests.

- **Engage with Students and Parents:** Discuss assessment results and learning goals with students and their parents/guardians. Be prepared to review and discuss these during the first monthly Umoja Team's Student Academic Observation meetings

Implementing Student Assessments

Our approach to student assessments began in 2009 when the Academy started administering the Northwestern Education Association (NWEA) standardized quarterly assessments to measure student progress. The assessment used was the Measure of Academic Progress (MAP), a computerized adaptive test that adjusts the difficulty of questions based on the student's performance on previous items. This test allows teachers to observe gains and losses at each grade level, identify students who need additional support, and tailor instructional strategies to align with specific learning objectives.

The "NWEA Results Fall 2009 – Spring 2010,"

The results from the 2009-2010 school year showed gains in mathematics across all grades, except for one grade 3 classroom and one grade 6classroom, as well as both 4th-grade classrooms. In reading, one 6th-grade classroom and the 7th grade did not show gains, while all other grades achieved gains ranging from 0.5% to 7.2%. To evaluate and enhance our instructional strategies, professional development programs were conducted during the summer of 2010 to determine what worked and identify areas for improvement.

Enhanced by new technology, the educational system began evolving to better support the required state curriculum. In August 2010, we designed and implemented a faculty retreat focused on using data to improve teaching effectiveness. We used "Leverage Leadership: A Practical Guide to Building Exceptional Schools" by Paul Bambrick-Santoyo, with contributions from Brett Peiser, as our guide.

Our strategy focused on having teachers use student assessment results to guide their instruction:

- **Adapting Teaching Strategies:** Modify teaching methods based on student assessments to enhance achievement, including approaches like project-based learning.
- **Implementing Whole Brain Teaching:** Incorporate techniques that engage the entire brain in the learning process.
- **Gesell Training and Team Building:** Participate in Gesell training and team-building exercises to strengthen collaboration and understanding.
- **Setting Teacher Goals:** Establish clear goals for teachers.
- **Developing Individual Student Learning Plans:** Create personalized learning plans for each student based on their unique needs and assessment results.

In the second year of the turnaround, the October 2010 MEAP test results, reflected that the "Percentage of Students Met or Exceeded MEAP Proficiency: 2009-2011." The report showed significant double-digit gains in reading and mathematics for 4th and 8th grades. While these achievements were noteworthy, they were overshadowed by declines in scores across all other grade levels compared to the previous test results.

The Michigan Educational Assessment Program (MEAP) was a standardized test. The test was taken by all public-school students in the U.S. state of Michigan from elementary school to middle / junior high school from the 1969–70 school year to the 2013–14 school year.

The Percentage of Students, at the academy, Met or Exceeded MEAP Proficiency: 2009 -2011

The leadership team saw a need to increase professional development, monitoring of curriculum and delivery of instruction. This was to ensure that all teachers had a firm grasp on the curriculum and new teaching strategies.

Again, during the summer of 2011, the leadership team assessed data relative to the school program, curriculum, delivery of instruction, and student achievement. When reviewing the NWEA and the MEAP results with the staff at the August faculty retreat, the team concluded that the students continued to require strong academic assistance and needed to stay on-track. The NWEA results for 2010 – 2011 indicate continued gains for all grade levels in mathematics, and all grade levels in reading except for grade 2.

Did the gains translate to improved student performance on the MEAP? A review of MEAP objectives, cut scores, and an individualized item analysis identifying missed GLCEs, along with classroom reports, led administrators to conclude that as the bar for MEAP proficiency had been raised, there was a need for enhanced teacher performance and innovations to further boost student achievement.

The adjustment involved daily monitoring of each classroom to observe the implementation of lesson plans, adherence to the written curriculum, and student response and progress. Additional time for reading and math was allocated through block scheduling, and professional development opportunities were aligned to ensure that teachers understood and confidently executed the new curriculum components.

The focus remained on teaching strategies that support the curriculum for mastery of the basics and the Michigan GLCEs.

The Academy, Expanded

During the third year of the turnaround, in September 2011, The Academy expanded to include 9th grade and relocated the 7th and 8th grades to join them at the new middle/high school campus, located two blocks from the K-6 elementary school. In prior to the September move, in June 2011, we hired five Teach for America teachers for the middle/high school, adding to the Teach for America teachers hired the previous year. These teachers were well-qualified, energetic, and effective, with a strong focus on student achievement and character development.CC

MEAP assessments were administered in October 2011. Criteria for determining proficiency was revised resulting in increased cut scores. Upon initial review of the demographic results, one would surmise that the achievement level for 2011 had declined significantly.

However, upon analyzing the mean scale scores for 2009, 2010 and 2011, students at every grade level in Reading experienced an increase in mean scale scores for 2011. Grade 3 experienced a significant increase of 20 points in achievement for reading while all other grades saw an incremental increase from 2 to 7 points.

The results of the Reading, *Mean Scale Scores* and *Percent of Students Meeting AYP at Levels 1 and 2* was apparent that there was a greater disparity between the percent proficient as opposed to the mean scale scores for 2010 and 2011. Yet, the mean scale scores indicate that The Academy had shown some improvement in Reading achievement.

The mean scale scores for mathematics reflected an increase in 2011 for grades 3, 4 and 6, however slight. Grades 7 and 8 show a slight decline of one point, each, while grade 5 reflects a decline of 89 points. The scores were not a surprise and were somewhat validated by the Ed Performance assessments, also administered in the fall.

The leadership team attributed the school's New Educational System's initiatives of Pattern Writing and the reading and writing process as instrumental in improving students' writing. Science results indicate no improvement in achievement, while social studies reflect a slight gain of 4 points in mean scale scores with a 23% decrease in the percentage of students meeting or exceeding proficiency

In response to the minimal progress being made in mathematics, the leadership team revised the scheduling to accommodate two mathematics classes per day. Teachers receive additional support in Math Corps and Singapore Math, as administrators monitored more closely to insure effective execution of the mathematics curriculum. Individual student data was reviewed and analyzed and individualized mathematics packets were prepared for students.

We also applied for and received a grant.

T.E.A.M. Project Grant Using Student Data to Inform Instruction

The grant provided us with an opportunity to enhance our use of student data to inform instruction. Brenda led the initiative, resulting in our selection by MAPSA in 2011 to participate in the T.E.A.M. Project through the Teacher Incentive Fund Grant. This project focused on increasing teacher effectiveness by utilizing student data to guide instruction. All Academy faculty received training through the grant on how to analyze and apply assessment results to improve instruction and boost student academic achievement. Additionally, a financial incentive was offered to teachers who successfully improved students' academic progress by leveraging data. This initiative was well-received by the teachers.

As part of the Teacher Incentive Fund Grant, the Academy purchased computers for the high school classrooms and adopted the Scantron Ed Performance Assessment along with the Northwest Educational Association (NWEA) tools.

Response to the Data

The variance in Ed Performance scores across categories highlighted a greater need for differentiation within instruction. When gains were consistent among high-achieving categories, but lower-achieving categories showed no improvement or even declined, it suggested that the instruction was not effectively targeting all achievement levels and learning styles.

To address this, intensive interventions were implemented to close the achievement gap in reading and mathematics. These interventions included individualized and small group instruction, utilizing existing curriculum programs such as Math Corps, Singapore Math, Study Island, and Zoo-Phonics. Progress monitoring was conducted four times a year using Ed Performance and Study Island.

Study Island was employed as a data-driven intervention due to its alignment with Scantron assessment objectives. Teachers could review Scantron assessment results, identify students' incorrect responses, correlate specific lessons and modules in Study Island with the Scantron objectives, and track students' progress.

Mathematics instruction continued to be held twice a day, with one class focused on mastering basic skills and the other on grade-level GLCEs. The increased use of technology and math manipulatives supported students in knowledge acquisition and performance. Schoolwide writing assessments were administered and collected in March, April, and May of 2012.

There was also an increased emphasis on vocabulary development, including context clues, etymology, and word stems. General and special education teachers collaborated to design packets for fluency and comprehension practice and met weekly to review student progress. "Marzano's Narrative Frame" and "Marzano's Nine" were integrated into professional development and classroom practices, along with "***Bloom's Revised Taxonomy***."

The Definition of Bloom's Taxonomy: "In one sentence, Bloom's Taxonomy is a hierarchical ordering of cognitive skills that can, among countless other uses, help teachers teach and students learn."

At the start of the second semester in January 2012, Magnum closely monitored the frequency of observations, teacher evaluations, and the use of data to improve instruction. Brenda provided Magnum with weekly status reports on the progress of staff instruction and student learning, based on her daily walk-throughs and observations.

The Umoja teams focused intently on identifying specific objectives that students had not mastered, aligning targeted instructional strategies and actions to address those objectives. To ensure continuous improvement and that students had highly effective teachers, Brenda was required to:

- **Conduct Walk-Throughs and Informal Observations:** Visit each classroom for 10 minutes daily—14 visits across K-6 (two classes per grade) and 12 visits for grades 7, 8, and 9 (covering ELA, Math, Science, and Social Studies for each grade).
- **Provide Feedback:** Use a duplicate form for each visit, with one copy for the teacher and one for the file.

- **Conduct Formal Observations:** Observe at least three teachers weekly, complete an observation feedback report, and follow up with a post-observation conference with the teacher.
- **Analyze Results:** Provide a detailed analysis of Scantron results within five days by class and subject, and within ten days by student.

It was Brenda's responsibility to ensure data accuracy, to make sure that teachers received and understood the results, and to conduct frequent formative assessments of each student in reading, writing, and math. This included administering a pre-assessment before each lesson or unit and a post-assessment afterward. ***www.hmhco.com › blog › what-is-the-purpose-of What Is the Purpose of Formative Assessment? | HMH,*** Aug 21, 2023.

The primary purpose of formative assessment was to inform teachers about whether students were learning the material taught during day-to-day classroom instruction. Some examples included exit slips, low-stakes quizzes, polls, think-pair-share activities, as well as digital tools for formative assessment.

The faculty was prepared to discuss the frequent assessment results, progress, or lack of progress of each student in the monthly Umoja Team's Student Observation meetings. Discussions also covered changes in teaching strategies based on the assessment results.

Daily quizzes were conducted to review the previous day's work, or five-a-day quizzes were used each day for the same purpose. Teachers were advised to enter notes, scores, and results into PowerSchool.

It is important to note, we were sensitive to no over testing the students . We made sure testing didn't dominate the calendar and culture of schools and cause undue stress for students and teachers.

Student assessment results were used to change, modify, or strengthen instructional strategies. All instructional strategies were based on student learning assessment results.

These elements interacted to inform teachers if they needed to change teaching strategies to enhance student learning. Instructors were advised to keep a portfolio of all students' assessment results, learning goals, and progress.

Teachers to Use Multiple Measures

We believed it was important for teachers to use multiple measures and indicators when assessing student learning and achieving success. For example, data from a single administration of a statewide reading or math test does not provide enough information to improve student learning. Similarly, relying on a single formative assessment to measure students' reading progress is not as reliable as using multiple, varied assessments to triangulate the complex concept of student reading.

It was extremely helpful for teachers to become knowledgeable about how to use summative assessment data, such as from initial student assessments, weekly assessments, yearly state tests, Study Island, project-based learning, the NWEA, and Terra Nova. Understanding how these results could best inform or improve teaching practices was crucial to enhancing student learning.

- **Summative Assessments:** These assessments offer data typically used to track student progress over time, indicating whether students are making the expected level of progress based on their age and abilities. (Third Space Learning)
- **Standardized Testing - NWEA:** Academy students in grades K-8 participated in NWEA tests in the fall and spring of each year. These tests measure what students already know in math and reading and what they still need to learn, helping teachers target instruction to each student's learning level. The spring tests assess each student's academic growth during the year.
- **Terra Nova Test:** We also supported the administration of the Terra Nova Test, an achievement test commonly given to students in grades K-12. It measures achievement in reading, language arts, mathematics, science, social studies, vocabulary, spelling, and other areas.

The Terra Nova Test is published by CTB/McGraw-Hill and has set the bar for the highest standards in research, item reliability and validity, and technical quality.

We ensured that testing did not overwhelm the school calendar or culture. We carefully balanced the testing schedule to prevent it from dominating the school environment, thereby minimizing stress for both students and teachers.

Setting Measurable Goals for Students

We instructed teachers to set targeted goals for each student in the classroom once they had key summative data. Teachers could use this baseline data to identify mastery levels and the learning needs of their class, demographic subgroups, and individual students.

With this information, teachers could set measurable weekly, monthly, and year-end instructional goals, which would serve as meaningful targets to guide their pedagogical strategies. These goals were designed to be Specific, Measurable, Attainable, Results-Oriented, and Time-Bound (SMART). An example of such a goal might be:

- The percentage of third-grade students scoring at Level 3 or higher on the state mathematics test will increase from 64% in Spring 2010 to 82% in Spring 2011.

Focus areas for improvement:

1. *Number sense*
2. *Computation*
3. *Measurement*

We emphasized to teachers that formalized goal setting could lead to improved student learning outcomes. All goals created by teachers in collaboration with administrators should include the following six components (with example language from the goal above):

1. A measurable baseline (64%)
2. A measurable target (82%)
3. A specific time frame (Spring 2010 to Spring 2011)
4. Specificity about what is being assessed (percentage of third-grade students scoring at Level 3 or higher)
5. Specificity about the method of assessment (the state mathematics test)
6. Focus areas that guide future action needed to reach the learning target (number sense, computation, and measurement)

These types of goals could be used with common assessments, teacher-made rubrics, and other types of assessments, as well as with standardized tests from publishing companies and state departments.

Frequent Student Assessments and Analyzing Formative Data

We instructed teachers to complete an assessment of students in their classrooms during the first week of school. We managed the testing schedule to maintain a balanced school environment, reducing stress for students and teachers. This gave teachers a good sense of where their students were at the beginning of the year and allowed them to set measurable goals for where they wanted the students to be by the end of the year. The early assessments provided a clear direction, and assessments throughout the year informed progress.

The next step for teachers was to implement a system of frequent formative assessments to benchmark the progress of their students during the school year toward those year-end goals. Simply using baseline data to set measurable year-end goals, without also implementing a system for frequent analysis and adjustment of instructional and organizational practices, was not likely to result in significant improvements in student learning.

Effective formative assessment practices, implemented during the school year, were shown to be a powerful mechanism for improving student learning. Research meta-analyses demonstrated that good formative assessment had a greater impact on student learning and on closing achievement gaps than any other instructional practice (see, e.g., Black & William, 1998).

Teams Academic Observation Student Meetings

To realize the instructional power of formative assessment practices, teachers needed the opportunity to meet regularly and frequently in their Umoja Team for collaborative, data-based discussions about student progress. During these meetings, teachers identified emergent patterns from the formative data and discussed what the data revealed about students' progress toward weekly, monthly, and year-end learning goals.

Teachers then collaboratively identified appropriate instructional interventions that could be implemented during the next instructional cycle and collectively committed to implementing those interventions. The regular student observation meetings that reviewed assessment results were shown to have major impacts on student achievement and teacher satisfaction.

Data Use to Facilitate Student Learning

The teacher's data analysis was meaningless if it did not lead to meaningful instructional changes. Teachers needed to use both summative and formative assessment data to implement strategic, targeted, and focused instructional interventions that improved student learning. These interventions had to be aligned with state standards and curricula, as well as content-specific and developmentally appropriate best practices.

Many teachers felt disempowered and fatalistic about their ability to significantly impact student learning outcomes. They believed that the academic success of their students and schools depended largely on the characteristics of the students and their families. However, other educators believed that by working collaboratively, they could have a powerful impact on student learning.

The latter group, who recognized their potential to make a difference and who were strategically and intelligently redesigning instructional and organizational practices to support student learning, were the ones closing achievement gaps and succeeding in this new era of accountability.

Schools that continued to struggle were those that placed the bulk of the responsibility for student learning—and the blame for the lack thereof—on students and families, rather than accepting that many classroom practices and school structures could be changed to better facilitate student achievement.

Student Data as a Form of Feedback

Data-driven teachers view data as feedback, not as indictments. They use data to inform pedagogical modifications and actively seek out more data to assess the success of those changes. Data-driven teachers are also willing to discuss their instructional strengths and weaknesses with peers in the Umoja teams, fostering shared communities of practice focused on individual student learning.

Confucius noted that "a journey of a thousand miles begins with a single step." While we may not be able to address the often-overwhelming problem of low student achievement all at once, we can take small steps that, together, add up to significant improvements over time. Using assessment data helps. We were on that journey with teachers at the Academy and believed we were making progress.

We believed that data-driven assessment and teaching would help teachers increase their effectiveness and ensure that their students were retaining what was being taught.

CHAPTER XXVIII
THE IMPORTANCE OF EFFECTIVE TEACHERS

We believed that training teachers in student-driven data instruction, brain-based learning, and teamwork skills would enhance their effectiveness in the classroom. Effective educators must also foster a positive learning culture and remain updated on the latest research and developments in education. It's essential for teachers to strive to be the best-trained professionals in their field.

Our research on effective teachers in urban schools, like the Academy, identified three key characteristics that are most directly related to teacher effectiveness in such environments.

These characteristics include self-awareness (intrapersonal skills), understanding the environment in which they teach, and maintaining high expectations for students. These were the traits we specifically sought in the Academy's teaching staff. Additionally, we evaluated how committed the teachers were to develop their professional skills, as opposed to those who saw teaching as merely a convenient job or did it because they liked students. We were also interested in their ability to work collaboratively as part of a team and whether they truly believed that all students can learn.

Furthermore, we believe that effective teachers should also demonstrate the following qualities:

- **Be aware of what they believe about the Academy children's capabilities.** Teachers should reflect on their own belief systems and assumptions, especially in instances where their social backgrounds and experiences differ greatly from those of the students they teach (Weiner 1993; 1999).
  That is why we preferred to hire African American teachers. They Teachers should know how their personal values influence perceptions and ultimately affect teacher expectations and practices (Diffily and Perkins 2002).
- **Effective teachers maintain high expectations for all students**, regardless of where they teach or the backgrounds of their students.
- **We stressed that teaching students is more than just a job, for pay and time off.** It is a profession we believe is to be the best educated teacher you can be, to share their knowledge and skills with students.
- **We advised staff to learn, grow, improve, become the best in their profession,** it benefits student learning. Isn't that what's it is all about.

More important than the curriculum is the question of the methods of teaching and the spirit in which the teaching is given. Bertrand Russel.

Understanding the significant impact that teachers' high expectations have on student success is crucial.

CHAPTER XXIX
PARENTAL INVOLVEMENT

Parent involvement had been one of our top priorities, with research demonstrating its significant impact on student outcomes. We introduced strategies to enhance teaching and learning, emphasizing the crucial role that parents play in supporting these efforts. At the Academy, we actively encouraged and supported parent participation. For decades, global research has shown that parental involvement—through parent-teacher conferences, school events, parent-teacher organizations, and at-home discussions about school—leads to higher academic achievement and improved social-emotional outcomes for students.

To foster parent engagement, we included a parent on the Academy's Board of Directors and invited grandparents to assist with tutoring. We developed a budget and designated a staff member to head the parent organization, ensuring they had support in planning and conducting meetings and receiving updates from the administration.

Parents Are Teachers Too (PATT) was the Academy's official parent involvement group, meeting the Title I Parent Involvement requirements. This group provided essential support to the Academy's leadership. Around 20–25 parents volunteered regularly, and PATT meetings typically saw participation from 30–40 parents. During these meetings, we discussed curriculum, assessment results, schoolwide test performance, and the overall school culture.

To further increase parent engagement, students performed at Family Night events, which significantly boosted attendance. The Academy also hosted various other activities, including Parent/Curriculum Night, parent workshops, parent-teacher conferences, monthly grade-level meetings, Annual Title I meetings, Open House events throughout the year, and the Scholastic Book Fair. Parents eagerly anticipated year-end community events, which celebrated their children's accomplishments. Staff members worked closely with parents to plan events for special occasions like Juneteenth and Kwanzaa celebrations.

PARENT PERCEPTION SURVEY – November 2011				
	Yes	Usually	Rarely	No
1. I am satisfied with the instructional program	72%	6%	9%	12%
2. I am satisfied with the amount of hands-on materials and activities provided.	64%	5%	5%	21%
3. It is good to have paraprofessionals to assist after school and with tutoring.	83%	12%		

4. I feel comfortable and safe at this school.	92%	7%		
5. My children have good relationships with the school staff and principal.	85%	8%	5%	3%
6. My family and I have good relationships with the principal and teachers.	80%			
7. What I like most about this school is the family environment	96%	3%		
8. What I like most is the African-centered education program.	90%	5%		4%
9. I am satisfied with the after-school programs.	65%	15%	4%	11%

Parents' Perception of the Academy

Overall, parents' perception of the Academy was very positive. The chart above indicates the results of the 2011 Parent Perception Survey. Parents appreciated the family atmosphere and the personal attention their children received. The administration worked collaboratively with parents to discuss and resolve their concerns. Parents also became involved with their children in a community project.

Parents and Students Involvement in the Community

The value and merit of the Academy to the community were considerable. For many years, the Academy was surrounded by abandoned homes—some burned out, some boarded up—which posed an imminent danger to the community and to children walking to and from school. Despite the best efforts of the principal and the parents, little was done to address the issue. During the 2009–2010 school year, an Academy digital media teacher engaged eighth-grade students and their parents in a service project.

The students took digital pictures of the vacant and boarded-up houses lining the streets near the school. Under the teacher's supervision, they prepared a media presentation, which they presented to the Detroit City Council. The Council applauded the initiative and creativity of the students. Within three months, the vacant and abandoned houses were torn down.

Each year, the students and parents planted and tended a garden, distributing free vegetables to parents, Genesis House, Operation Get Down's halfway house, and the wider community. During the summer, students assisted staff in preparing the vegetables and enjoyed eating them with their parents.

Community Service and Partnerships

The Academy had a strong foundation in community service. It conducted two annual drives to support the homeless and those in need: an annual hats and gloves drive, and a food and blanket drive. Additionally, the Academy partnered with Bed, Bath & Beyond to provide parents with bedding, baby clothing, furniture, household appliances, and more. Parent volunteers delivered food and refreshments left over from programs and school activities to shelters and halfway houses.

The former Southeastern Village initiated in 1991 was a collaborative effort between the Detroit Public Schools and several organizations with long-standing histories of serving youth and families on Detroit's east side. This initiative aimed to improve the quality of life for children and families in the community bounded by Mack Avenue, the Detroit River, Mt. Elliott, and Alter Road. Southeastern Village played a vital role in supporting the Academy from 2002 to 2014, providing essential services and resources to both parents and students.

Alkebu-Lan Village, founded in 1978 with the original goal of offering affordable martial arts training to Afrikan American youth, later expanded its offerings to include youth and adult sports, fitness, leadership training, visual and performing arts, homework assistance, tutoring, youth entrepreneurship training, and community service. Alkebu-Lan Village has provided after-school and summer programs for Academy students, including tutoring, martial arts, gardening, and dance. The center also offered bus transportation for students.

Alkebu-Lan Village continues to provide educational, cultural, and recreational programs to over 1,000 Detroit youth and their families annually through both on-site and outreach programs. The Academy benefited greatly from its productive relationship with the Village, local businesses, and community members. These local businesses regularly donated and supported the Academy's various programs and activities.

In addition to business support, vendors and neighbors contributed to community service projects initiated by the Academy, such as neighborhood and citywide clean-up drives and food and blanket distribution efforts. Faith-based partnerships also played a significant role, offering mentoring and tutoring support. One key partner, Renaissance Unity Church in Warren, Michigan, provided mentoring and tutoring during school hours, as well as donating books for the school library and backpacks for students.

The business community viewed the school as a cornerstone in the local area and a key communication link for new community-building projects.

CHAPTER XXX
REFLECTIONS BY BRENDA AND WARRINGTON

Warrington with a few of the students at the Academy

We Assisted the Academy, in Enhancing and Providing Quality Education

We supported the Academy in its efforts to enhance and sustain a high-quality education by implementing a strategic turnaround process, fostering a supportive school culture, and strengthening community and parental involvement."

The turnaround process was guided by a diverse skill set Bernard, the Academy's founder and CEO, utilized his experience as a community organizer, while Brenda and I applied our expertise in organizational psychology, education, and leadership. This experience marked a pivotal moment in our ongoing dedication to serving others and enhancing the lives of underserved communities. During our time at the Academy, we successfully assisted in renewing the school's charter for an additional five years and supported students in achieving success on state-wide tests

Bernard's request for us to assist with the Academy's turnaround process provided Brenda and me with a meaningful opportunity to give back to our community, bringing our journey full circle. Having grown up in the neighborhood, we were honored to contribute to the community that helped raise us.

Our time at the Academy in Detroit was one of the highlights of our lives. We are deeply honored that Bernard entrusted us with this important task, and we will always hold this experience in the highest regard. The school community became like family, and the students like our own children. We were dedicated to their success and committed to putting in the time and effort needed to ensure it.

In my work at the Academy, Warrington focused on supporting male students at high risk of street influences. With Bernard's help, he secured jobs for them around the school, attended their football games, and aimed to serve as a role model. Redirecting their energy away from the streets was challenging, but it was a mission both were deeply committed to.

Brenda concentrated on improving literacy among middle school girls, many of whom were reading at a third-grade level or below. She engaged the girls by introducing them to books on Kindle via iPads. They eagerly met three times a week at 7:30 in her office, and they were always punctual. Their reading and comprehension skills improved significantly.

One of the greatest challenges the Academy faced was gaining acceptance as a public charter school due to its unique focus on an African-Centered curriculum. Its goal was to teach students about their African American history, heritage, and culture—an aspect not included in the Detroit Public Schools curriculum. The Academy needed to integrate state-required educational standards with lessons on African American culture, ideals, values, and history. Established to provide high-quality, African-centered learning experiences for children and families in the surrounding African American communities. The Academy aimed to boost Black students' confidence and self-esteem and academics. It successfully fulfilled this mission.

We have always believed, and reminded our students, of B.B. King's saying, 'The beautiful thing about learning is that nobody can take it away from you.' We continue to learn alongside our students tin order for them to be better equipped to serve others. As the saying goes, 'Each one, teach one'—a principle we embrace for the betterment of society. The appendices supporting this book provide further details.

CHAPTER XXXI
SUMMARY COMMENTS

Bernard Parker, Jr, the CEO of Timbuktu Academy

In 2005, I appointed a principal with a robust academic background in African-centered education, including a Ph.D. in the field, though they lacked significant administrative experience. Unfortunately, this decision led to a noticeable decline in our academic performance from 2006 to 2008, with the Academy failing to meet statewide achievement benchmarks. By 2009, it became apparent that Timbuktu Academy was deteriorating, not only academically but also in terms of our standards, discipline, teacher commitment, and our dedication to African-centered education.

Recognizing the need for substantial intervention, I found myself uncertain about the best course of action. The looming threat of state closure or plummeting enrollment added to the urgency. In search of guidance, I traveled to Sedona, Arizona, to consult with my cousin Warrington and his wife Brenda, affectionately known as Gigie. Their extensive experience in education and organizational psychology seemed particularly pertinent to our situation. Brenda's background as a seasoned principal and administrator, combined with Warrington's Ph.D. in organizational psychology and his success in corporate turnarounds at Rockwell International, provided a wealth of expertise.

During our discussions, Brenda and Warrington concurred that a comprehensive assessment of the school was essential to identify the underlying issues. Following this assessment, both the principal and the board chairperson resigned, leaving us in desperate need of new leadership. After some hesitation, I asked Brenda if she would temporarily assume the role of principal until a permanent replacement could be secured. I fully understood the magnitude of this request, as Brenda and Warrington had retired and were relishing their dream life in a new home on a golf course in Sedona. To my astonishment and profound gratitude, Brenda agreed to take on the role, with Warrington offering his support in the school's turnaround efforts.

In 2009, Brenda and Warrington embarked on their transformative work at Timbuktu Academy. They conducted workshops, provided teacher training, and thoroughly revised the curriculum. Their efforts extended beyond academics, as they worked diligently to rebuild relationships with both staff and students, emphasizing the importance of mutual respect and appreciation. This holistic approach necessitated some difficult personnel changes, but it ultimately revitalized the school's culture.

Over the next three years, the turnaround was nothing short of remarkable. Enrollment increased, standardized test scores improved, and, most significantly, the attitudes of parents, students, and teachers became overwhelmingly positive. This collaborative effort culminated in a successful transformation of the school.

As of 2024, the positive changes initiated by Brenda and Warrington continue to benefit Timbuktu Academy. Their expertise and willingness to sacrifice their retirement years were instrumental in saving the school, and I remain deeply grateful for their contributions. Words cannot adequately convey my appreciation for the pivotal role they played in revitalizing Timbuktu Academy.

I hope that this book will serve as a valuable resource for schools in need of turnaround strategies or for those just wanting to improve their schools.

THE AUTHORS

Bernard F. Parker, Jr.

Bernard Parker, CEO of Magnum Educational Management Company, which manages the Academy, is a former community activist, director of Operation Get Down (OGD), and Wayne County Commissioner. He has deep roots in the community, having grown up on the east side of Detroit. Bernard attended Catholic schools and pursued higher education at Highland Park Community College and the University of Michigan.

Hired by the United Methodist Church as a Black Community Developer, Bernard became passionately committed to improving his community. In 1970, he co-founded Operation Get Down, an organization that allowed him to engage in all aspects of community work and build partnerships with businesses, government, education, and faith-based institutions. His dedication to families on Detroit's east side led him to collaborate with Dr. E. Malkia Brantuo.

The late Dr. E. Malkia Brantuo, who joined OGD after working with Detroit Public Schools (DPS), was profoundly influenced by her more than 36 visits to Africa. These experiences gave her a cultural baptism into her African heritage. As a Pan-Africanist, Dr. Brantuo was convinced that African American children would benefit greatly from an African-centered educational environment and curriculum.

Bernard hired Dr. Brantuo to oversee OGD's adult education program. In 1980, OGD opened the Ujima Childcare Center to serve local children, providing an African-centered, child-focused program grounded in the seven principles of Nguzo Saba and a commitment to academic excellence. The success of these ventures led to the founding of Timbuktu Academy as a private school in 1996. However, the school soon closed due to a lack of funds, as many parents were unable to pay tuition. Determined to continue their mission, Commissioner Parker and Dr. Brantuo sought to reopen Timbuktu Academy as a charter public school.

Brenda A. Parker, BA, MFA

Head of Timbuktu Academy, and Superintendent (2009-2013)

Education:

- University of Michigan – Bachelor of Arts in Education with Distinction

- Carnegie Mellon University, Pittsburgh, PA – MFA in Fibers
- University of Pittsburgh – Graduate Studies in Education and Art History

Administrative Educational Experience:

Brenda has over 27 years of experience as a school principal and administrator. She served as principal for 16 years at two different private independent schools in Los Angeles, CA. During her tenure, she was responsible for designing and developing highly successful, diverse, and child-centered educational environments.

Classroom Teaching Experience:

Brenda's teaching career spans over 25 years, working as an instructor across various educational levels. She has taught students from preschool through ninth grade, covering early childhood, elementary, middle, and secondary education in both public and private schools. Additionally, she is trained as a reading specialist.

Publication

Still Waters, published on Amazon, June 2024.

Warrington S. Parker, Jr., Ph.D.

Organizational Psychologist

Education and Experience:

Warrington has over 30 years of experience in education and business. He earned his Ph.D. in Organizational Psychology and an MA in Psychology from the University of Michigan. He also holds a BA in Sociology and a Michigan Teaching Certificate. His teaching experience spans the elementary, secondary, and adult basic education levels. Additionally, he served as a professor at the University of Michigan's School of Management (Dearborn Campus) and as an adjunct professor at Wayne State University in Detroit, Michigan.

Business Experience:

Warrington has extensive experience in the business world, having worked for Rockwell Corporation as an internal organizational change agent for over 25 years. Rockwell, a high-technology company serving the aerospace, defense, communications, and automotive industries, provided a platform for his expertise in organizational change and executive leadership development.

His contributions to the development of high-performance organizations were featured in Industry Week in the article "**Rockwell's Bold New World**" (1987). Additionally, he led the redesign of Bellflower High School in Bellflower, CA.

Academic and International Experience:

Warrington also served as an adjunct professor at the Korean University for Brain Education in Mokehon, South Korea, and was Vice President of the International Brain Education Association. He has worked and presented at the United Nations in New York. Together with his wife, Brenda, he helped organize and present at the International Brain Education Conference at the United Nations. They also played a key role in establishing a Korean NGO at the UN and spoke with ambassadors from El Salvador and Africa about gang violence and the potential of Brain Education training.

Current Role:

Recently, Warrington was the Program Director and a professor for an online master's degree program in *The Science of Regenerative Earth Management,* based in Arizona. He has also lectured in the People's Republic of China.

After Rockwell:

Following his retirement from Rockwell, Warrington and his wife founded a consulting company, The Warrington Group.

Publication and scheduled for publication

- *Strength of Will: A Memoir,* published on Amazon in January 2024.
- *Cracking the Rock,* scheduled for publication in November 2024, which details his experiences as an internal organizational change agent at Rockwell Corporation.
- *U-Turn, Timbuktu Academy an African-Centered Public Charter School in Detroit.* To be published in November,2004.

APPENDIX A
GUIDELINES FOR AFRICAN CENTERED EDUCATION

At Timbuktu, We Believe:

- Schools have the responsibility to create environments where every child can learn according to their unique abilities.
- All children have the right to a high-quality education.
- Every child is capable of learning.
- Dedication, practice, and commitment are key to educational and personal development.
- Schools should prepare children for both social and academic success.
- Schools should offer an enriched and challenging curriculum aligned with the State's Core Curriculum, while also integrating African and African American history and culture through research.

Our Vision:

- To build and maintain a model African-centered institution rooted in integrity, where we holistically nurture the development of critical thinkers who use science and technology to enhance the quality of life for families and communities around the world.

Our Mission:

- To engage students, families, teachers, and the community in creating a holistic approach to learning that equips students with a strong academic foundation, applied scientific knowledge, and moral education through a rigorous African-centered curriculum. Social, cultural, and physical activities will be integral components of the learning experience.
- At Timbuktu, teaching and learning will be grounded in integrity, emphasizing.
- constructive, applied knowledge, and focusing on core competencies and critical thinking to foster the development of the whole child.
- Several foundational concepts have shaped Timbuktu Academy since its inception, while others have been integrated over time. Below are definitions of these guiding principles.

Mama or Baba:

- At the Academy, children refer to adults as "Mama [name]" or "Baba [name]." "Mama" means mother, and "Baba" means father. We use these terms because we see ourselves as extensions of the family, caring not only for the academic development of the children but also for their overall growth as human beings.

African-centered Education (ACE):

- African-centered Education (ACE) is a holistic system of educating the entire family, rooted in the best of African cultures and traditions. It involves collaborative learning, diverse instructional methods, and extended learning opportunities. ACE places the African child at the center of all learning, recognizing that African children thrive when they are loved and feel a strong connection to their school and teachers.

ACE is built on the belief that all children can learn, and that African children will excel when high expectations are set, and when they are instilled with the confidence that nothing is beyond their ability to achieve. ACE is guided by the ancient principles of MAAT. Ma'at was an Ancient Egyptian Goddess, but she was also a concept or principle, of justice or 'right attitude'. Egyptians worshipped Ma'at by living life according to the principles of Truth, Justice, Righteousness, Order, Balance, Harmony, and Reciprocity.

Principles of Ma'at:

Represents the weighing of the soul in ancient Kmt (KMT is the name for the country that was used by the Ancient. African people in what we now call Egypt. It means "the black land" or "the black people of the land.")The heart of the deceased was believed to be the seat of the soul and was weighed on the scale of Ma'at against a feather, which symbolized truth and righteousness. This symbolic weighing determined the righteousness of the deceased.

According to Dr. Theophile Obenga, Ma'at is a concept of central importance, encompassing order, universal balance, cosmic regulation, justice, truth, truth-in-justice, rectitude, and moral uprightness. The concept of balanced order forms the permanent basis of pharaonic civilization, bringing peace and condemning crime and evil. Those who break the law are punished accordingly.

To understand Ma'at, one must examine it on multiple levels:

1. **Universal Level:** Ma'at expresses harmony of the elements.
2. **Political Level:** Ma'at works against injustice.
3. **Individual Level:** Ma'at embraces specific rules for living in concert with moral principles.

Living according to the rules and principles of Ma'at leads to achieving universal order in one's own life. The principles of Ma'at include:

- Truth,
- Justice,
- Righteousness,
- Order,
- Balance,
- Harmony,
- Reciprocity

Nguzo Saba: represents seven fundamental values of African culture that contribute to the strengthening and reinforcement of family, community, and culture among African American people and Africans worldwide. Developed by Dr. Maulana Karenga, these values form the core of Kwanzaa's origin and meaning, serving as essential building blocks for community development and empowerment. **The Seven Principles are:**

- **Umoja (Unity):** To strive for and maintain unity in the family, community, nation, and race.
- **Kujichagulia (Self-Determination):** To define ourselves, to name ourselves, to create for ourselves, and to speak for ourselves.
- **Ujima (Collective Work and Responsibility):** To build and maintain our community together, making our brothers' and sisters' problems our own and solving them together.
- **Ujamaa (Cooperative Economics):** To build and maintain our own stores, shops, and other businesses and profit from them together.
- **Nia (Purpose):** To make our collective vocation the building and development of our community, restoring our people to their traditional greatness.
- **Kuumba (Creativity):** To do as much as we can, in the way we can, to leave our community more beautiful and beneficial than we inherited it.
- Imani (Faith): To believe with all our heart in our people, our parents, our teachers, our leaders, and the righteousness and victory of our struggle.

Various Swahili Words Used in Unity Circle and Protocol:

Below is a list with explanations of these terms:

- **Angalia:** A Swahili verb meaning "look, watch, observe." We use "angalia" to denote a position assumed when standing at attention. Sisters cross their arms over their chest with the right arm over the left, fists in the Black power position. Brothers fold their arms across their chest (right over left) with elbows extended.
- **Asante (sana):** When thanking someone, we say "Asante." Adding "sana" emphasizes the phrase, making it "thank you very much." The response is "karibu," meaning "don't mention it / no problem."
- **Hodi hodi:** This word means "hello!" and is used instead of knocking before entering a room. Before entering, everyone (children and adults alike) should call out "hodi hodi" and await the response of the mwalimu.

- **Jambo: Hell**
- **Karibu: "Karibu"** means "welcome" and is the response a mwalimu will give to indicate that a person may enter the room.
- **Mwalimu:** This word means "teacher." When referring to more than one teacher, use "walimu."
- **Umoja, mbili, tatu, Anzeni!:** Translated as "1, 2, 3, begin," this phrase is used during Unity Circle to prepare participants to begin the next part all at the same time.

(1.0) Obenga, T. (2004). African Philosophy: The Pharaonic Period, 2780-330BC. (Ayi Kwei Armah, Trans.). Per Ankh (Original work published 1990).

APPENDIX B
UJIMA (COLLECTIVE WORK AND RESPONSIBILITY) ACTIVE COOPERATION

In the context of community social order, cooperation is a key aspect of Ujima. It emphasizes that actions taken to benefit others ultimately benefit oneself. This idea aligns with the Yoruba proverb, "One who injures others, in the end, injures him/herself." Similarly, in the Ubuntu community of South Africa, children are taught not to be aggressive or competitive, but to be cooperative and to share responsibility as a fundamental moral obligation.

They believe that "if people do not agree, there can be no relationship." Moreover, if people must be coerced, there cannot be genuine agreement. In such a context, collective work and responsibility are naturally facilitated and sustained.

APPENDIX C
HAPPY. TEACHERS MAKE HAPPY STUDENTS

Written By, Warrington S. Parker Jr, PhD, and Brenda A. Parker, BA, and MFA.

The Academy is a K-8 public charter school in Detroit, grounded in an African-centered educational philosophy. Located in the heart of the city, the school serves 351 students, all of whom are African American, with over 95% qualifying for free or reduced lunch. The goals of this philosophy are to instill pride, foster self-determination, build character, and produce well-educated students.

Timbuktu Academy successfully met its Annual Yearly Progress (AYP) target in 2010. Given the brain's essential role in learning, behavior, and emotions, it is crucial for educators to understand how the brain functions. By adopting a brain-friendly "Happiness School" culture and educating teachers on how students' brains respond to various social interactions, we have seen significant improvements in student learning and behavior.

Faculty and staff receive regular training in these areas, with periodic sessions conducted throughout the school year. Research on brain function, especially in the context of learning and social interactions, suggests that it is possible to shift a school's culture, improve student behavior, and enhance the academic focus and overall functionality of an inner-city school.

Faculty trained in Brain Education designed and led staff training sessions to create a brain-friendly "Happiness School" culture. This approach integrates a caring yet firm discipline, high expectations, belief in the students, recognition of each student's potential, and personal connections with them.

Our experience has shown that fostering a caring and personal connection with each student positively impacts their brain development, learning, and behavior. Faculty were introduced to "whole brain teaching," which emphasizes the use of multisensory techniques in instruction. They also learned about the crucial role that social interactions in the classroom play in shaping student behavior, attention, and openness to learning.

A key focus of the training was understanding how a Happiness School culture supports students' brain health and overall well-being.

Happiness School Culture

The **Happiness School** culture encourages faculty and staff to maintain a positive attitude, smile, and uplift students. They are expected to greet students and parents warmly each morning and eliminate hostility and yelling. This uplifting atmosphere has a positive effect on student well-being.

Key tenets of the Happiness School culture include:

- Creating safe, caring, loving, and orderly school and classroom environments as the norm.
- Building powerful connections with each student and knowing them well.
- Encouraging a happy smile on everyone's face at all times.
- Fostering calm, caring, and respectful interactions with students.
- Valuing the rights and comfort of others as a daily practice.
- Celebrating a sense of humor.
- Promoting student learning, happiness, health, self-esteem, self-confidence, and inner peace through the curriculum and teaching strategies.

This **Happiness School** culture has a profound positive impact on students' brains, improving behavior, increasing motivation to learn, reducing discipline issues, and boosting overall classroom success. It is essential for administrators, teachers, and staff to build strong personal connections with each student, demonstrate care, and avoid expressing anger. Students are more likely to listen to teachers when they feel genuinely cared for.

Inner Peace We also wanted the staff to have inner peace.

Internally happy people are the ones who can regulate how they feel, regardless of what's going on around them. They can make themselves happy and don't have to wait around for the world to give them a good day. When you find your inner happiness, you will achieve an emotional balance. It's essential to learn to rely on yourself in life. This state of life for teachers can have a powerful impact on students learning and behavior.

www.powerofpositivity.com › inner-happiness-why-it-matters

The power of personal bonding helps students release their defensive postures and enhances their internal motivation to learn and succeed. This motivation grows stronger when their successes are acknowledged and recognized by peers, parents, or guardians. The combination of a teacher's personal connection and the recognition of a student's achievements contributes to increased self-esteem, self-confidence, and a sustained motivation to learn. Ultimately, students develop an "I can do it" attitude.

Personally, Connecting to Students

The brain is inherently social, and the way educators interact with students significantly impacts their receptiveness to attention and learning. When administrators and teachers connect with students on a personal level, show care, and offer support and praise, they trigger the release of serotonin in students' brains. This neurotransmitter promotes a sense of well-being, regulates mood, and helps alleviate anxiety and depression.

Serotonin opens students' minds to new ideas and fosters a desire to engage with and support their teachers. When students feel good about themselves, endorphins are released, helping them relax and improve their overall mood. Conversely, when teachers or administrators' express anger, verbally berate, or reject students, this "social pain" can be as damaging as physical pain, according to human-performance researcher David Rock.

Such hostility often leads to student disengagement, classroom disruptions, and a lack of motivation. Additionally, when students perceive unfair treatment, their brains release cortisol—a hormone necessary for normal metabolic function but harmful in excess. Elevated cortisol levels can cause the brain to shut down, closing students off to new ideas and reducing their willingness to learn.

The Brain's Social Nature: Its Impact on Student Behavior and Learning

The brain is a social entity that thrives on interaction and collaboration with others for growth, learning, and survival. Some neuroscientists, as David Rock notes, view the human brain as having a social network responsible for interacting with the social world, much like networks responsible for movement, vision, thinking, and memory.

This social brain network allows us to understand and connect with others, as well as to regulate our own emotions and behavior. The quality of interactions between teachers and students, or parents and children, has a profound impact on the brain. Social interactions are often perceived as either fair or unfair, which in turn influences behavior, motivation, performance, and learning.

Research shows that the brain places intrinsic value on fairness. Functional MRI scans reveal that when individuals perceive fairness, the brain's reward centers are activated, much like when seeing a loved one or tasting delicious food. Fair treatment can foster positive self-esteem in students. Conversely, perceptions of social unfairness trigger heightened activity in the amygdala—the brain's "fear circuitry"—leading to feelings of anger or disgust. According to Rock, one study found that fairness was more important to the brain than money.

Fairness in social interactions also helps build personal connections and bonds between teachers, parents, and students, addressing their social needs. When these needs are met, it leads to improved classroom management and performance. When unmet, it can introduce feelings of threat and conflict.

Basic social needs that impact behavior at school or home include the need for connection and bonding with parents, teachers, and friends; a sense of fairness, status, safety, certainty, and autonomy; and the ability to make choices and decisions. These needs are fulfilled or unfulfilled through social interactions in the classroom, at work, at home, and in society. Meeting these needs leads to effective classroom dynamics and improved performance, while unmet needs can lead to conflict and disruption.

APPENDIX D
THE BRAIN IN SCHOOL AND AT WORK

**Written By, Warrington S. Parker Jr, PhD, and Brenda A. Parker, BA, and MFA.
This article was influenced by our experiences at the Academy.**

Introduction

> *"From the brain and the brain alone arise our pleasures, joys, laughter, and
> jests, as well as our sorrows, pains, and griefs."* — Hippocrates.

In the past 10 to 20 years, a wealth of research has emerged from neuroscientists, psychologists, and cognitive scientists. These researchers have been able to map what happens in the brain during thinking, learning, motivation, stress, emotions, and social interactions. Their work has shed light on the brain's role in shaping human behavior, employee performance, and student learning.

Thanks to advancements in technologies like functional magnetic resonance imaging (fMRI), which measures blood flow in the brain; electroencephalography (EEG), which tracks electrical activity; and positron emission tomography (PET), which creates images of brain activity, we've experienced a neuroscience boom. Researchers have used these technologies to study neural connections in various parts of the brain while people engage in different activities.

These research findings have provided valuable insights into how humans think, learn, feel, act, and perceive the connection between the brain and body. The studies have had practical implications for leaders, teachers, administrators, parents, and employees, helping them understand what it takes to bring out the best in students, colleagues, and themselves.

Many of these lessons were derived from studies conducted by neuroscientists, psychologists, and cognitive neuroscientists, as discussed by experts such as Rock (2010), Ratey (2008), Medina (2008), the OECD (2007), and Goldberg (2001). These findings have helped individuals in schools, homes, and workplaces better understand their own brains, improve social interactions, boost motivation, and enhance performance.

Interestingly, many neuroscience discoveries about behavior and learning reinforce what leaders, teachers, and parents have long suspected about student and employee motivation. However, now these ideas are backed by brain research. If the role of teachers, leaders, and parents is to influence behavior and open minds, shouldn't they understand how the brain functions?

About the Brain

Before diving into the lessons, a brief overview of the brain and its relevant parts will be provided. This discussion offers only a glimpse into what is currently known about the brain.

Our brain sets us apart from other species, allowing us to accomplish extraordinary feats such as building space shuttles, walking on the moon, and creating masterpieces in literature, art, and music. It enables us to engage in moral reasoning, rational thought, memory, emotion, and learning.

The human brain—a spongy, three-pound mass of fatty tissue that resembles a cauliflower—has often been compared to a supercomputer. However, it is far more complex than any machine, a fact scientists continue to discover with each new breakthrough.

While the full extent of the brain's capabilities remains unknown, it is the most intricate living structure in the universe. This single organ controls essential bodily functions like heart rate, breathing, digestion, and blood circulation. It is also believed to influence the immune system's response to disease and even affect how well individuals respond to medical treatments.

Beyond these vital functions, the brain shapes our thoughts, hopes, dreams, and imaginations. It organizes and mediates all human behavior, whether in school, at home, or at work. In essence, the brain is what makes us human (Medina, 2008).

More specifically, the brain contains between 1 billion and 100 billion neurons—cells that transmit information to other nerve cells, muscles, or glands. Neurons are the brain's working units, forming what is known as the brain's "gray matter." These neurons gather and transmit electrochemical signals through a vast network of nerve fibers called dendrites and axons, which make up the brain's "white matter."

The brain's interconnected structure, with neurons forming pathways through dendrites and axons, enables its remarkable functionality. These billions of nerve cells are produced, grow, and organize into efficient systems that typically function throughout a person's lifetime. Learning and memory processes are rooted in these interconnecting neuronal networks.

The brain's capacity for learning depends on the number of neurons and the richness of the connections between them. Functionally, the brain is highly specialized, with different regions responsible for specific tasks. These regions work together, aided by chemical messengers called neurotransmitters, to perform various functions (OECD, 2007; Arnsten, 1998; *Society for Neuroscience, 2008).*

The Brain, Plasticity and Continuous Learning

Neuroscientists widely agree, with a vast body of data confirming, that our brains are flexible. This flexibility, known as plasticity, is what enables learning. As a result, leaders, employees, students, teachers, and parents—all human beings—can change their brains and continue learning throughout their lives.

The brain's ability to adapt to environmental demands, learn, and change over a lifetime is a key aspect of plasticity. Initially, it was believed that only infant brains possessed this flexibility, due to the rapid growth of new synapses in babies' brains, which coincides with their acquisition of new skills (OECD, 2007). Synapses are small gaps between the axon of one neuron and the dendrite of another, where signals are transmitted, facilitating communication between brain cells (neurons).

According to Hebb's insight (1949), learning occurs when new experiences and challenges cause neurons to grow new dendrites, forming connections with other neurons. With new learning and experiences, we can continue to grow synapses throughout our lives. As Goldberg (2009) explains in Brain World, this process involves the ongoing growth of small blood vessels that supply the brain and the creation of new synapses—and in some cases, new neurons—in certain areas of the brain.

In his work, Goldberg (2001) identifies three essential elements needed to activate neuroplasticity and stimulate true learning:

1. **Challenging Activities**
   For mental activities to effectively stimulate neuroplasticity, they must be challenging. Whether in the classroom or the workplace, teachers, leaders, and parents need to present new concepts or tasks that are difficult but achievable. The challenge should push individuals beyond their mental autopilot—a state in which they perform tasks effortlessly based on past experiences.

2. **Novelty**
   The activities must also be novel. New brain cells grow, and neural connections form when existing brain networks are insufficient to handle the new task. This is why exposure to genuinely new information or experiences—ones that stretch beyond familiar comfort zones—is crucial for learning.

3. **Diverse Mental Activities**
   To maximize the benefits of neuroplasticity, mental activities should also be diverse. The brain consists of various specialized regions, each responsible for different tasks. Just as different muscle groups are activated during physical exercise, different parts of the brain are engaged by varied mental activities. The more diverse the challenges, the more the brain benefits from experience-driven neuroplasticity.

We are capable of learning new things for a lifetime through these novels, challenging, and diverse experiences. Teachers, parents, and leaders can help others change their brains by designing learning experiences that incorporate these three elements.

Moreover, individuals can take control of their own brain development through self-directed neuroplasticity (Rock, 2010), rewiring their brains through intentional actions and choices. Thanks to the brain's remarkable plasticity, no one is bound by habitual behaviors, lack of motivation, poor performance, or negative emotions. Every person has the innate ability to change their own brain by embracing new learning opportunities and experiences.

The Brain, Learning New Behavior, and Accepting Change

Getting employees, leaders, students, parents, and teachers to change behavior, learn new material, or accept information that contradicts what they already know requires significant mental effort and energy. There is a strong tendency to stay on autopilot, which may explain why change is often resisted, even when the change could be beneficial.

The prefrontal cortex, located just behind the forehead, is where information from experiences is first processed and temporarily stored as "working memory." This region of the brain is responsible for generating our own thoughts, holding them without external input, and processing moment-to-moment information from our environment. It also plays a crucial role in decision-making, problem-solving, predicting future events, and making self-directed choices. However, despite its importance, the prefrontal cortex has its limitations—it can only hold a small amount of new information at any given time.

To make learning stick or change behavior, the prefrontal cortex must transfer working memory information to the basal ganglia, a group of nuclei located at the base of the brain and attached to the brain stem. The basal ganglia are where habits are stored after repetitive tasks. This area is associated with motor control, cognition, emotions, and learning (Rock, 2010). When a task or lesson is repeated often enough, it becomes automatic and gets embedded in the basal ganglia.

Throughout the day, as students learn or process new information, earlier learned information can be replaced or lost in the prefrontal cortex. To prevent this, teachers, parents, or supervisors must design strategies that reinforce the material. This can be done by making the information repetitive, presenting it in a familiar context, making it novel and challenging, or diversifying the mental activities. Without these strategies, the limited capacity of the prefrontal cortex may lead to the information being lost.

David Rock (2008) explains that this is why employees often revert to habits stored in the basal ganglia—the part of the brain responsible for routine activities, like driving to work on autopilot. Learning new information or changing behavior requires new mental effort, which can be energy-intensive. Many people are reluctant to expend this energy unless the incoming information can be easily compared with what is already stored in the basal ganglia.

For learning or behavior change to occur, students and employees must do the hard mental work of comparing new information with what is already known in their brains. If there is little to compare the new information with, they are likely to reject it, opting for the familiar over the unknown.

Therefore, it is crucial for teachers to connect new information to what students already know, making it more relatable. Additionally, the information must be repeated at least three to four times to embed it in long-term memory within the basal ganglia. It's also important to engage the limbic system, the brain's emotional center, since emotions play a significant role in capturing attention, increasing memory retention, and leading to deeper learning.

The Brain, Student Attention, Learning, and Retention of Information

In *Brain Rules* (2008), Medina asks, "Does it matter to learning if we pay attention?" His answer is a resounding "Yes." When a student or employee's brain is fully engaged, they will never forget the experience. The more attention the brain pays to a given stimulus, the more deeply the information is encoded and retained in the basal ganglia. This has significant implications for teachers, student learning, and employee performance.

The Brain and Better Attention Equals Better Learning

There is a well-documented link between attention and learning, as research shows that better attention always results in better learning, regardless of whether it's in an eager kindergartener or a bored middle school student (Medina, 2008). Improved attention enhances retention of reading material, clarity in writing, and performance in math and science—across all academic areas.

Since attention is a critical factor in learning, teachers and employers must find ways to capture and maintain attention to facilitate meaningful learning. Medina notes that students and employees begin to lose attention after about ten minutes. Neuroscience suggests that the brain shuts off after a certain amount of time, limiting how much information can be processed and learned in one sitting. Peer-reviewed studies support this claim, showing that students often mentally disengage before a lecture or presentation is even halfway through.

What happens at the 10-minute mark to cause this? According to Medina, nobody knows for sure, but it seems the brain follows a stubborn timing pattern, influenced by both culture and genetics.

The Brain, Movement, and Exercise on Student Learning

It's important for students to stand up, move around, and engage in short exercises to stay fully engaged during a class. Long lectures where students sit for 45-50 minutes often lead to little or no learning. While a teacher may feel they've done their job by delivering information, passive listening does not guarantee active learning.

The Brain, Listening, Attention, Memory, and Learning

When students listen to a teacher, millions of sensory neurons in their brains fire simultaneously, each carrying messages and competing for attention. However, only a few of these messages will break through to the student's awareness, while the rest will be partially or completely ignored.

Messages that capture a student's attention are linked to memory, interest, awareness, and emotions. Often, what students pay attention to is influenced by their previous experiences, which help them predict where to focus. Interest and importance are tightly connected to attention. The brain continuously scans its surroundings, assessing events for personal relevance. The more relevant something is, the more attention students will give to it.

The Brain, Emotions, Student Attention, and Learning

Emotionally charged events are better remembered than neutral ones. Memorable or even distressing events activate the brain's amygdala, the region responsible for forming and storing memories associated with emotions. When the amygdala is triggered, it releases dopamine, a neurotransmitter that enhances memory and information processing. This mechanism acts like the brain putting a "Remember this!" note on the information, ensuring that the emotionally significant material is retained. This is precisely what every teacher and parent hopes for.

The Brain, Neuroscience, and the Practice of Mindfulness for Optimal Student Learning.

Mindfulness is a secular practice that helps students improve academic performance by creating optimal learning conditions in the classroom. It reduces student stress, enhances emotional coping skills, improves sustained attention, and fosters better behavior, concentration, focus, and empathy.

As described by the Mindful Schools Organization (2015) in Oakland, CA, and similarly by Jan Chozen Bays (2011), "Mindfulness is deliberately paying full attention to what is happening around you and within you—in your body, heart, and mind—without criticism or judgment." This realization can significantly benefit classroom learning conditions and the overall school environment.

The most common definition of mindfulness comes from Jon Kabat-Zinn, Ph.D. (1995), a leading expert in the field and founder of the Center for Mindfulness at the University of Massachusetts Medical Center in the 1970s. He describes mindfulness as a particular way of paying attention in the present moment without judgment, noting that the beneficial effects of mindfulness are well-documented scientifically.

Over the past two decades, research into the neuroscience of attention and emotion has profoundly impacted education. It is now widely acknowledged that children and adolescents need programs to develop their social and emotional intelligence, as well as their ability to regulate stress, attention, and emotion. Mindfulness practices in schools have proven to be effective in helping students develop these skills while creating optimal learning conditions.

The Neuroscience of Mindfulness in Education

Neuroscience has become one of the strongest supporters of mindfulness practices in schools. Research shows that children living in chronic poverty, experiencing long-term stress, often endure "amygdala hijacks." This constant fight-or-flight response negatively affects their learning and school experience.

The amygdala, part of the brain's limbic system or emotional center, reacts almost instantly when it perceives danger or stimulation, much like when you think you've seen a bear or tiger. It then takes two to three times longer for this signal to reach the prefrontal cortex, the brain's "thinking" area, where the situation is evaluated. The prefrontal cortex then sends a signal back to the amygdala with the message, "Relax, there's no danger."

Mindfulness practices have been shown to calm the amygdala, allowing children to pause before reacting negatively. This gives the prefrontal cortex enough time to positively engage and evaluate the situation. The prefrontal cortex is responsible for many executive functions, such as decision-making, critical thinking, working memory, social interactions, and integrating cognition with emotion.

Research has shown that children living in chronic stress conditions experience detrimental effects on brain development, particularly in the prefrontal cortex. However, mindfulness practices can counter these effects, enhancing critical thinking, reducing negative emotional responses, and improving decision-making.

Neuroplasticity and Mindfulness

The brain has an inherent ability called neuroplasticity, which allows it to change the way it thinks and processes information. Mindfulness practices can physically alter the brain in positive ways, improving children's behavior, reducing negative emotions, increasing attention and focus, and fostering better decision-making. Ultimately, these changes create optimal learning conditions for students.

Extensive research reveals that regular mindfulness practice in schools—even just a few minutes a day—can significantly improve students' self-control, classroom participation, and sense of respect for others. It also promotes internal happiness, optimism, and self-acceptance.

Mindfulness and Emotional Regulation

Emotionally charged events tend to be better remembered than neutral ones. When the brain detects such an event, the amygdala releases dopamine, a neurotransmitter that facilitates memory formation. This process acts like a mental "sticky note," ensuring that the information is remembered.

Mindfulness practices have been shown to help calm the amygdala and allow the brain's executive functions in the frontal cortex to take over, leading to more thoughtful responses instead of reactive behaviors. These practices have also been found to improve students' attention, emotional regulation, and social-emotional intelligence, creating a more positive learning environment.

Ratey (2008), in Spark: *The Revolutionary New Science of Exercise and the Brain,* states that exercise improves learning on three levels:

Optimizing Mindset: Exercise enhances a student's mindset, improving alertness, attention, and motivation.

Cellular Basis for Learning: It prepares and encourages nerve cells to connect with one another, a crucial step for students logging in new information.

Development of New Nerve Cells: Exercise spurs the development of new nerve cells from stem cells in the hippocampus, a part of the limbic system responsible for long-term memory and spatial navigation.

Research shows that incorporating physical education, movement breaks, recess, and energizing activities into the school day is an effective cognitive strategy. These activities strengthen learning, improve memory retention, and enhance student motivation and morale.

The Brain is Social: How Types of Social Interactions Make a Difference

The human brain thrives on social interaction. Students—and people in general—require interactions with others for learning and survival. The type of interactions in schools and workplaces can have different effects on the brain. Some interactions can be perceived as social pain, fairness, or unfairness, and these perceptions can influence motivation and learning.

The Brain, Social Pain, and Its Impact on Students and Employees.

When students or employees are berated or rejected by a teacher or supervisor, their brain experiences this rejection as social pain, which can feel as harmful as physical pain. According to David Rock (1980), such experiences can lead to demotivation, disengagement, and a "don't care" attitude.

The Brain, Social Fairness, and Its Impact on Students

Research shows that the brain inherently values fairness. MRI scans reveal that when people perceive fairness, the brain's reward centers light up—like seeing a loved one or enjoying good food. Fair treatment can enhance self-esteem and positive feelings at school or work, positively impacting motivation.

Conversely, feelings of unfairness can trigger the brain's fear response, leading to disgust and resentment. Rock (1980) notes that one study found fairness to be more important to the brain than money.

Social fairness can promote learning and enhance both student and employee motivation. When teachers or leaders show genuine interest, care, and support, they trigger the release of serotonin in the brain, which opens individuals' minds to new ideas and fosters a desire to connect and cooperate.

The Brain and the Effects of Demotivation on Students

If teachers or leaders diminish students or employees, it triggers the release of cortisol, a stress hormone that shuts down cognitive processes and receptivity to new ideas. This can lead to demotivation, absenteeism, disengagement, or even dropping out of school.

The Brain and the Effects of Status Differences

Significant status differences between students or employees can be perceived as unfair. Schools and organizations that work to minimize status differences often see increased learning and a greater willingness to achieve goals.

The Impact of Expectations on the Brain

Cognitive research shows that expectations can physically impact the brain. "Expectations can determine whether we see or don't see information," says Rock (1990). One study found that warning a patient that a stimulus would hurt less reduced their pain rating as much as a dose of morphine. The power of expectations can shape how the brain processes information.

Meeting Expectations and the Brain's Response

When students' or employees' expectations are met, their brains release dopamine, which is crucial for clear thinking and motivation. Conversely, when expected positive outcomes are not realized, dopamine levels drop, leading to disappointment and reduced motivation.

Expecting Negative Outcomes or Facing Uncertainty and the Brain's Response

If students or employees expect negative outcomes, their dopamine levels drop further, which impairs decision-making and problem-solving. The brain prefers predictability, and even mild uncertainty—such as not knowing if a word is on a page—can trigger stress responses that impair cognitive functions. Larger uncertainties, like test stress or potential layoffs, can overwhelm the brain and diminish decision-making abilities.

Sleep, the Brain, and Learning

To optimize brain function and retain learning, students and employees need sufficient sleep. "If you have learned a lot of information and sleep on it, you can wake up with better insights into what you have just learned," says Ed Boyden, Ph.D., of MIT. Sleep is essential for consolidating learning into long-term memory.

APPENDIX E
THE EFFECTS OF PROLONGED CHRONIC STRESS. IMPLICATIONS FOR STUDENT LEARNING AND BEHAVIOR

Warrington S. Parker Jr, PhD, and Brenda A. Parker, BA, and MF

(Article influenced by the authors experience at Timbuktu Academy,
an African-Centered Detroit Public Charter School) Warrington
S. Parker Jr, PhD, and Brenda A. Parker, BA, and MFA

Introduction

Teachers in schools serving students from inner-city environments, where prolonged poverty is common, often experience frustration, as many have expressed at Timbuktu Academy of Science and Technology (TAST). Despite these challenges, the teachers at TAST are hardworking, dedicated, and committed to improving the academic performance of their students.

Timbuktu, a K-8 Detroit Public elementary charter school, has been in operation for the past thirteen years. In September 2011, the school expanded to include a high school, starting with the 9th grade, with plans to add one grade per year until it serves students through the 12th grade.

Timbuktu Academy of Science and Technology (TAST) is located on the east side of Detroit and consists of two buildings: a middle/high school building and an elementary school building, both within walking distance of each other. Combined, the elementary and middle/high schools serve 443 students, with over 95% of the student body qualifying for federal free and reduced lunch programs. The surrounding neighborhood is marked by vacant lots, abandoned or burnt-out houses, and high crime rates. Despite these challenges, the core mission of the school remains centered on student learning and teaching.

Teachers

Teachers working in schools located in neighborhoods like Timbuktu, where many students experience prolonged poverty, often express concerns about chronic tardiness, high absenteeism, lack of motivation to study, low academic achievement, and inappropriate social and emotional behavior. Additionally, many educators report that students frequently act out, use profanity, appear to lack self-discipline, and are highly emotional—quick to fight and show disrespect toward both teachers and peers.

These complaints and frustrations are common among many teachers who work with economically and socially underserved students. Often, educators in inner-city schools attribute their students' low academic achievement and disruptive social and emotional behavior to parents or guardians and the home environment. It is frequently said that parents or guardians do not read to their children, encourage reading, or provide enriching mental experiences. Additionally, they are often blamed for not disciplining their children or creating a home environment conducive to supporting social and academic development, with little attention to positive role modeling.

There may indeed be a connection between the home environment and the experience of chronic stress, starting as early as the prenatal period and continuing through early childhood (up to 24 months). Recent neuroscience research has revealed the negative impact of living in profound poverty and enduring chronic toxic stress on children's brain development. This stress can severely affect both learning and behavior.

Purpose

The purpose of this article is to share with teachers, parents, and school leaders the recent research findings on the negative effects of prolonged poverty, chronic stress, and poor nutrition on three critical parts of children's brains, and what can be done at school and home to reverse these effects. The three brain areas affected are the prefrontal cortex, the hippocampus, and the amygdala. Damage to these parts of the brain may help explain why children exhibit disruptive social and emotional behavior, poor memory, delayed cognitive development, and low academic achievement in school.

There is a range of early social, emotional, and material deprivations that impact the structural and functional organization of the brain, as well as socio-emotional development, both postnatally and throughout childhood. However, children are not permanently bound by the brain damage caused by their circumstances of poverty. Thanks to the brain's neuroplasticity—its intrinsic ability to adapt and change—there is potential for recovery and growth and change the brain for a lifetime.

This article will conclude with a discussion about the various strategies that can be used at home and in schools to reverse the brain damage caused by the stress of children living in prolonged poverty. The research results could alter classroom educators and school leader's approach to students and their teaching strategies. A few words about poverty in the United States.

Just two generations ago, policymakers, school leaders, and teachers often viewed children raised in poverty with sympathy, but without fully understanding how deeply their circumstances diminished their chances for success (Jensen, 2009). Today, a wide body of research clearly highlights the significant impact poverty has on children's brain development. Furthermore, we now have evidence that schools can achieve student success with economically disadvantaged students.

Given this knowledge, we can confidently say that there is no excuse for allowing any child to fail, regardless of their home situation. It is essential for parents, educators, and school leaders to better understand the effects of poverty and chronic stress on children's brain development and collaborate to reverse these effects. A critical first step in this process is understanding what is meant by poverty.

Jensen (2009) explains that the word *poverty* stirs strong emotions and raises many questions. In the United States, the official poverty thresholds are set by the Office of Management and Budget (OMB). Individuals whose income is insufficient to meet basic needs—such as food, shelter, and clothing—are classified as poor. However, the cost of living varies dramatically by location; for instance, someone classified as poor in San Francisco might not be considered as poor if they lived in Detroit, Michigan.

The "absolute poverty line" is defined in the U.S. as the threshold below which individuals or families cannot meet their basic needs for healthy living, having insufficient income to provide essential food, shelter, and clothing to maintain health.

Jensen (2009) defines poverty as a chronic and debilitating condition resulting from multiple adverse synergistic risk factors, affecting the mind, body, and soul. Although poverty is complex and does not look the same for everyone, the recent research on poverty, stress, and poor nutrition shows that these conditions negatively affect brain development.

When parents, teachers, and school leaders gain a deeper understanding of how poverty, prolonged stress, and poor nutrition affect the brains of children and teenagers, they can modify their teaching strategies and child-rearing practices to help students mitigate some of the brain damage caused by these conditions. In the following section, we will review research studies on the effects of poverty on children's brain development.

Research Studies on Poverty and Children's Brain Development

Emerging research on the effects of poverty on children's brain development, including studies by Harris (2006), Evans and Lee Vincent (2009), Evans and Schamberg (2009), Jensen (2009), Gianaros (2010), and Farah (2010), indicates a strong positive correlation between prolonged poverty, high stress levels, and negative impacts on a child's brain development, starting from an early age.

These early experiences often result in social and emotional behavioral issues and poor academic performance later in life. While many poor children show resilience and can overcome significant obstacles, poverty still poses a serious threat to healthy brain development. Evans and Lee Vincent (2009) suggest that growing up poor isn't just difficult for children—it may also be harmful to their brain development.

In fact, a 2008 study published in the *Journal of Cognitive Neuroscience* found that the neural systems of children from impoverished backgrounds develop differently compared to those of middle-class children. This difference represents a physiological or neurological effect on the brain that begins in early childhood and can manifest in school performance, continuing into adolescence and adulthood.

Next, we will discuss the brain development of infants living in poverty.

Infants in Poverty and Brain Development

Jensen (2009) argues that infants growing up in poverty often form weak or anxious attachments, which become the basis for full-blown insecurity during early childhood and manifest in the classroom.

Very young children require healthy attachments, opportunities for learning, and exploration for optimal brain development. Unfortunately, impoverished families tend to face adverse factors such as teen motherhood, depression, and inadequate healthcare. These challenges lead to decreased sensitivity toward infants (van Ijzendoorn et al., 2004), resulting in children facing emotional and social instability as well as poor behavior and academic performance in school.

Moreover, if a mother is abusing drugs, under tremendous stress, or facing physical abuse before a child is born, these factors may further contribute to the lack of social and emotional support after birth.

Harris (2006) suggests that the complex web of social relationships children experience early in life—with family members, peers, and adults at school—exerts a much greater influence on their brains and behavior than previously assumed. This process begins with the core relationships children form with their parents or primary caregivers, shaping a personality that is either secure and attached or insecure and unattached. Securely attached children, from birth to 24 months, generally behave better in school (Blair et al., 2008).

Starting at birth, the attachment formed between parent and child predicts the quality of future relationships with teachers and peers (Szewczyk-Sokolowski, Bost, & Wainwright, 2005). It plays a leading role in the development of social functions such as curiosity, emotional regulation, independence, and social competence (Sroufe, 2005). Infants are biologically hardwired for six basic emotions: joy, anger, surprise, disgust, sadness, and fear (Ekman, 2003). To develop the emotional and social tools necessary for healthy growth, children need the following:

- A strong, reliable primary caregiver who provides consistent and unconditional love, guidance, and support.
- Safe, predictable, stable, nurturing, and loving environments.
- Ten to 20 hours each week of harmonious, reciprocal interactions—known as attunement—especially critical during the first 6–24 months of life to help develop a wider range of emotions, including gratitude, forgiveness, and empathy.
- Enrichment through personalized, increasingly complex activities.

Children raised in poverty are far less likely to have these essential needs met compared to their more affluent peers, which can lead to serious consequences. Deficiencies in these areas inhibit the production of new brain cells, disrupt the maturation process, and alter healthy neural circuitry, undermining emotional and social development and predisposing children to emotional dysfunction (Gunnar, Frenn, Wewerka, & Van Ryzin, 2009; Miller, Seifer, Stroud, Sheinkopf, & Dickstein, 2006).

The importance of human contact and warmth is well established. A study of infants in Irish foundling homes in the early 1900s found that of the 10,272 infants admitted to homes with minimal or absent maternal nurturing over a 25-year period, only 45 survived. Most of these survivors grew into pathologically unstable and socially challenged adults (Joseph, 1999).

In many poor households, parental education is inadequate, time is limited, and warm emotions are rare factors that jeopardize the attunement process (Feldman & Eidelman, 2009; Kearney, 1997; Segawa, 2008). Caregivers in these environments are often overworked, overstressed, and authoritarian with children, employing harsh disciplinary strategies learned from their own parents. These caregivers frequently lack warmth and sensitivity (Evans, 2004) and fail to form solid, healthy relationships with their children (Ahnert, Pinquart, & Lamb, 2006).

Parents living in prolonged poverty often suffer from diminished self-esteem, depression, and a sense of powerlessness and inability to cope. These feelings can be passed on to their children through insufficient nurturing, negativity, and a general failure to meet their needs. A study on the emotional problems of children with single mothers found that the stress of poverty increases depression rates among mothers, leading to a higher use of physical punishment (Keegan-Eamon & Zuehl, 2001).

Children themselves are also vulnerable to depression; research indicates that poverty and prolonged stressors are major predictors of teenage depression (Denny, Clark, Fleming, & Wall, 2004). What are some of the chronic stressors children living in prolonged poverty may face?

Chronic Stressors and Children's Brain Development

In addition to the effects of weak social and emotional attachments between parents or guardians and children early in life, which can cause brain damage, children living in prolonged poverty often experience several chronic stressors. Jensen (2009) reports that these chronic stressors, which may place children at risk for brain damage, academic failure, poor performance, and emotional and behavioral issues in school, include:

- Very young, single, or low-education-level parents
- Poor nutrition
- Parents/guardians facing chronic unemployment
- Abuse, neglect, or substance abuse in the household
- Dangerous neighborhoods
- Homelessness and mobility
- Exposure to inadequate educational experiences

Chronic stress is an ongoing state of physiological arousal, occurring when children face many stressors like those mentioned above. They remain in a constant state of stress and feel they have no control over their circumstances. Their autonomic nervous system rarely has the chance to activate the relaxation response. While humans are built to handle short-term stress (acute stress) for brief periods, prolonged chronic stress can wear down the body and cause brain damage, as well as emotional and physical illness.

Children experiencing chronic stress can suffer negative impacts on the parts of the brain responsible for memory, language, reading, and overall cognitive development, which are essential for success in school.

Children's cognitive development is critical for academic success, and it is affected by chronic stress. One of the first studies examining cognitive responses to chronic physiological stress in children living in poverty was conducted by Evans and Lee Vincent (2009) and published in the *Proceedings of the National Academy of Sciences.*

Their study indicated that chronic stress from growing up in poverty has a physiological impact on children's brains, impairing working memory and diminishing their ability to develop language, reading, and problem-solving skills. Professor Gary Evans, of the Departments of Human Development and Design and Environmental Analysis, led this study. Evans stated, "There is a lot of evidence that low-income families are under tremendous amounts of stress, and we already know that stress has many implications. What these data raise is the possibility that stress is also related to cognitive development."

Evans and Michel Schamberg (2008), who worked with Evans, gathered detailed data on 195 children from rural households above and below the poverty line over 14 years. They quantified the physiological stress each child experienced at ages 9 and 13 using a "stress score" called allostatic load, which combines measures of stress hormones (cortisol, epinephrine, norepinephrine), blood pressure, and body mass index.

At age 17, the subjects underwent tests to measure working memory, which is essential for everyday activities and long-term memory formation. Evans found that children who lived in impoverished environments for extended periods had higher "stress scores" and suffered greater impairments in working memory as young adults. Those who spent their entire childhood in poverty scored about 20 percent lower on working memory than those who were never poor.

"When you are poor, when it rains, it pours," Evans explained. "You may have housing problems, more family conflict, and more pressure in paying bills. You're probably moving more often, which produces stress in families, including on the children." Evans concluded that chronic elevated stress is likely a contributing factor to the link between poverty and deficits in working memory.

The negative effects of poverty and chronic stress on children's brains are reinforced by Dr. Peter Gianaros's (2009) research at the University of Pittsburgh. His research using brain imaging shows that living in poverty can damage specific areas of the brain responsible for memory, attention, stress regulation, and delaying gratification. It may also hinder overall intelligence.

Martha Farah, Director of the Center for Neuroscience and Society at the University of Pennsylvania, is one of the leaders in the study of poverty's effects on the brain. In a 2006 research article, she argued that cognitive neuroscience could provide a framework for understanding and solving issues like the persistence of poverty across generations. She noted that this field is rapidly developing, moving from a lack of knowledge a few years ago to having a growing number of studies today.

In one of Farah's research projects, her team found that kindergartners from low-income families showed poorer function in the parts of their brains responsible for reading, language, and executive control compared to their middle-class peers. Executive control skills include working memory and impulse control—abilities crucial for success in school and social interactions.

It is critical for parents, teachers, and school administrators to understand which parts of the brain are affected by chronic, prolonged stress in children living in poverty.

Three Parts of the Brain Affected by Chronic Stressors

Chronic stress has a physiological impact on children's brains, particularly affecting and damaging the prefrontal cortex, hippocampus, and amygdala (Evans and Lee Vincent, 2009; Jensen, 2008; Farah, 2009).

- **The prefrontal cortex,** located at the front of the brain behind the forehead, is responsible for executive functioning, such as problem-solving, decision-making, planning, thinking, short-term memory, goal setting, social control, and suppressing urges that might lead to socially unacceptable outcomes.
- **The hippocampus** is part of the limbic system, often referred to as the "emotional brain." It plays a crucial role in managing emotions, consolidating information from short-term memory to long-term memory, and is essential for learning and memory.
- **The amygdala,** also part of the limbic system, helps process emotions and is heavily involved in managing the body's response to fear and stress. It is responsible for determining how to respond to events that produce an emotional reaction, such as emergencies or startling occurrences.

As a result of chronic stress, the negative impacts on these three parts of the brain impair children's working and long-term memory, attention in class, decision-making, goal setting, planning, and their ability to develop language, reading, and problem-solving skills.

- Chronic stress also has a profound impact on children's cognitive abilities, social and emotional behavior, academic performance, life/coping skills, and socio-emotional trauma, all of which negatively affect their learning and daily life management. Scientists believe that stress:

- Changes the activity of neurotransmitters (chemical messengers) in the brain's prefrontal cortex, hippocampus, and amygdala.
- Suppresses the creation of new neurons (brain nerve cells) in these three parts of the brain.
- Causes neurons (brain cells) to undergo negative remodeling of dendrites. Dendrites are part of the brain's communication network.
- Shrinks the volume of the prefrontal cortex and hippocampus, the areas most associated with working memory.

The way stress affects the brain and body explains why it wreaks such havoc. When a child perceives a threat—whether physical or emotional—the sympathetic nervous system triggers a cascade of signals that lead to the release of adrenaline from the adrenal glands. This increases blood glucose and fatty acid levels, providing energy to the muscles for fighting or fleeing from the stressor.

Breathing, heart rate, and blood pressure increase so that the muscles receive as much oxygen and nutrients as possible. Simultaneously, other hormones slow down or stop non-essential functions such as growth, reproduction, and immune response.

If the stressor persists, the adrenal glands release cortisol. Cortisol is intended for short-term stress, such as escaping a dangerous animal. However, when a person endures chronic stress (like the stress associated with poverty), the prolonged presence of cortisol can damage brain cells.

The hippocampus, which is crucial for learning and memory, is particularly vulnerable to cortisol and suffers the most damage. "Too much cortisol can prevent the brain from laying down new memories or accessing existing ones." Additionally, chronic cortisol exposure can hinder the development of the hippocampus, which may explain why children living in poverty often show poor functioning in memory-related brain regions.

Chronic stress can also damage the brain in other ways. During a stressful event, blood is diverted to the muscles, reducing blood flow to the hippocampus and other brain areas that are not essential for survival. This lack of energy impairs faculties like memory formation, language development, and future planning. Stress also alters the levels of dopamine in the prefrontal cortex, impairing its function in higher-level decision-making and planning, potentially leading to poor choices that hinder success in school or work.

Finally, chronic stress decreases the blood-brain barrier's ability to protect the brain from toxins, viruses, and other harmful agents. This increases the risk of brain damage, which can further impede academic and work success.

In addition to the damaging effects of chronic stress on a child's brain, poor nutrition can also negatively affect brain development, academic achievement, and social and emotional behavior. Research clearly shows that children's nutrition has a direct influence on their brain development.

Nutrition and Children's Brain Development

Research on the brain indicates that the foods children eat—or do not eat—affect their brain development, functioning, and behavior. Chemicals released in response to both stress and certain foods can inhibit higher-order thinking. Children living in poverty are often exposed to high levels of stress, and their nutrition may be poor. Chronic stress depletes the body of essential nutrients, inhibits the growth of dendrites, and limits the connections between neurons.

The result is that nutrients are unavailable for learning; thinking slows, and learning is impaired. Protein-rich foods, often lacking in the diets of impoverished children, release tyrosine into the bloodstream when digested. Tyrosine is converted into L-dopa in the brain and then into dopamine, which promotes feelings of alertness, attentiveness, quick thinking, motivation, and mental energy. However, fear of failure, isolation, and trauma—common in poor children—cause dopamine to convert into norepinephrine, which turns alertness into aggression and agitation.

Therefore, when nutrition is poor, children struggle to tolerate frustration and stress, become apathetic, and may exhibit non-responsive, inactive, and irritable behaviors (Given, 1998). How can they be expected to learn under these conditions?

Given (1998) also discusses the role of serotonin, carbohydrates, and their effects on brain functioning. Carbohydrates stimulate the production of serotonin. Low serotonin levels are associated with depression and low self-esteem. Additionally, the body produces serotonin when individuals experience positive self-esteem, success in problem-solving, and other accomplishments.

One implication for teachers is the importance of finding ways to ensure that all students experience success, thereby increasing serotonin levels. Another implication is ensuring that students have access to breakfast and lunch programs, as well as nutritious snacks.

Based on these research studies, children growing up in prolonged poverty, experiencing chronic stressors and poor nutrition, suffer damage to at least three parts of their brains. These children do not choose to behave differently in school; rather, they face overwhelming challenges that affluent children rarely encounter. Their brains have adapted to suboptimal conditions, affecting the prefrontal cortex, hippocampus, and amygdala in ways that undermine emotional regulation, social behavior, and academic performance.

A few significant risk factors identified by Jensen (2009) for children raised in poverty—which should be understood and addressed by teachers, parents, and school leaders—include:

- Emotional and social challenges, including a lack of emotional and social skills.
- Frequent exposure to prolonged stressors.
- Cognitive difficulties leading to low academic achievement.
- Health and safety concerns.
- Difficulty paying attention, concentrating, and focusing in the classroom.
- A tendency toward anger, emotional outbursts, and fighting.
- Disrespectful behavior toward teachers and peers.

There are teaching strategies that can be incorporated to help children in high-poverty communities overcome these challenges.

Teaching Strategies to Address Children's Needs

The combination of factors that underserved students face presents extraordinary challenges to their academic and social success. However, this reality does not mean that success is impossible. On the contrary, a deeper understanding of these challenges can help educators take specific actions to support less-advantaged students.

The good news is that brain development issues caused by chronic stress can be reversed through intensive interventions, both at home and in the school environment. Despite the grim realities, there is a silver lining. Understanding how the brain functions and how it is affected by prolonged poverty and chronic stressors can greatly influence how teachers approach the emotional, social, cognitive, and physical learning needs of students living in poverty.

This awareness enables educators to become more attuned to their students' emotional, social, and physical needs. Children who lack emotional and intellectual development may struggle with language acquisition, which in turn hampers the development of higher-order thinking skills necessary for independent problem-solving.

Parents who understand the effects of poverty on their children's brains and can provide consistent, nurturing care—along with addressing emotional, social, and physical needs—can mitigate many of the negative impacts of financial hardship, food insecurity, and lack of safety that often characterize impoverished childhoods.

In school, teachers can help by first addressing students' social, emotional, and physical needs. Building strong, personal relationships with each student, validating their experiences, actively listening to them, and giving them a sense of control over their learning process can significantly enhance their ability to succeed.

Teachers should maintain high expectations for students, employ hands-on learning strategies, connect academic content to students' experiences, and provide a warm, nurturing, and safe environment. In this way, they can counteract many of the negative effects of chronic stress on the brain. Additionally, teachers can focus on building the following core skills to help repair the damage caused by stress:

- Teaching students how to pay attention and focus in class.
- Exposing children to multi-sensory early learning experiences, such as patterning, sorting, classifying, sequencing, using number games, and exploring shapes.
- Modeling proper social and emotional behavior in the classroom.
- Repeating lessons and providing mental enrichment to support short- and long-term memory development.
- Encouraging problem-solving, perseverance, and the ability to apply skills in the long term.

For children living in high-stress environments, classrooms should maintain an atmosphere of "relaxed alertness." A safe, trusting environment can reduce stress and enhance learning. Classrooms should be high in challenge and low in threat, as fear and threat can cause the brain to downshift—a biological response that focuses solely on survival needs.

Children living in prolonged poverty often experience helplessness, low self-esteem, and fatigue, which makes downshifting more likely. In such cases, students will focus only on survival needs, blocking out new information and experiences. Repeated thoughts or unresolved emotional issues will dominate their attention, and the stress hormone cortisol will increase, resulting in emotional volatility.

Downshifting can also lead to behaviors such as hypervigilance, resistance, or defiance. Students in this state can only learn through concrete methods, not abstract ones, which should be considered when planning lessons and managing the classroom (Caine, 2000).

Cooperative learning and shared decision-making can help build a sense of community, fostering strong student-teacher and student-student relationships. This sense of belonging and connection can be especially beneficial for students from poverty, helping them feel more engaged with their school (Kovalik and Olsen, 1998). Additionally, helping students manage strong emotions productively can enable them to cope with feelings such as anger, fear, hurt, and tension in their daily lives and relationships. Once students can manage these emotions effectively, they will be free to learn.

Brain-based research supports the constructivist theory of learning, where students build understanding based on prior knowledge and experiences. Intellectual development is gradual and depends on external stimulation. If children experience deprivation, as is often the case with children in poverty, their intellectual development may be delayed.

Another key teaching strategy for high-poverty schools is the practice of Mindfulness. Teachers are encouraged to learn this method before implementing it in the classroom. Based on the author's personal experience with this practice for over 10 years, consistent practice (at least three times a week for 30 minutes) is essential. We will begin by defining the practice of Mindfulness.

What is Mindfulness?

Mindful Schools Organization (2015) in Oakland, CA, describes Mindfulness as a secular practice that helps students improve academic performance by creating optimal learning conditions in the classroom. This is achieved by reducing student stress, increasing emotional coping skills, improving sustained attention, enhancing student behavior, concentration, and focus, and fostering a deeper sense of empathy toward others.

Similarly, Jan Chozen Bayes (2011) defines Mindfulness as "deliberately paying full attention to what is happening around you and within you—in your body, heart, and mind. Mindfulness is awareness without criticism or judgment." This realization can be incredibly beneficial for students, supporting an optimal learning environment in school.

The most widely recognized definition of Mindfulness is offered by Jon Kabat-Zinn, PhD (1995), a leading expert in the field and founder of the Center for Mindfulness at the University of Massachusetts Medical Center in the 1970s. He describes Mindfulness as a specific way of paying attention in the present moment, without judgment.

He emphasizes that the benefits of Mindfulness practices are scientifically well-documented. Mindfulness, practices in schools are guided by a structured curriculum and teacher training, such as those developed by Mindful Schools Organization and the South Burlington School District in Vermont. Understanding the neuroscience behind Mindfulness is key to appreciating its impact on students.

Neuroscience, the Brain, and the Practice of Mindfulness

Two decades of research into the neuroscience of attention and emotion have laid the foundation for transforming modern education. It is now widely recognized that children and adolescents require programs that develop their social and emotional intelligence, as well as their ability to regulate stress, attention, and emotions. Mindfulness practices in schools have been shown to assist students in developing social-emotional intelligence, reducing stress, and controlling emotions.

Neuroscience research strongly supports Mindfulness practices in schools. Studies have shown that for children living in prolonged poverty and chronic stress conditions, the amygdala—the brain's emotional center—can become hijacked, keeping some children on high alert, which negatively affects their school life.

The amygdala is part of the limbic system, responsible for the brain's emotional responses. When a perceived danger or stimulation occurs, the amygdala reacts almost instantaneously, much like reacting to a bear or tiger. However, it takes two to three times longer for the message to reach the thinking brain (the prefrontal cortex), where the situation is evaluated, and then back to the amygdala, where the message "relax, there's no danger" is sent.

Mindfulness practices help calm this area of the brain. As a result, students learn to pause before reacting negatively, giving the prefrontal cortex time to send a "no danger" signal to the amygdala. This process engages the frontal cortex in a positive manner, which involves executive functions like decision-making, critical thinking, working memory, social interactions, and integrating cognition and emotion. The frontal and prefrontal regions of the brain activated during Mindfulness practices are critical for students' interpersonal and intrapersonal development.

Research shows that chronic stress negatively affects brain development, particularly in the frontal cortex. Mindfulness practices, however, have been shown to increase critical thinking, slow the amygdala's activity, and generally slow the mind-body response. When students become aware of the pause between a stimulus and their response, their brain changes, allowing responses to replace reactions.

The brain has an inherent property called neuroplasticity, meaning it can change the way we think and process information. Mindfulness practices can physically alter the brain in positive ways, improving behavior, reducing negative emotions, decreasing fight-or-flight responses, and increasing students' ability to pay attention, listen, and make better decisions.

Studies of successful implementation of Mindfulness practices in schools highlight its role in creating optimal learning conditions. Key lessons include starting with faculty training, setting clear goals for the practice, communicating effectively with parents, and setting a regular time for Mindfulness practice each day.

Mindfulness, when practiced regularly, can be a powerful tool in helping students from low-income backgrounds overcome the challenges they face.

Conclusion

The school leadership and teachers can design the school program to teach the core skills that will help with improving the damage to the brain and meet the other needs of students living in poverty. They can focus on the basics of reading, math and writing for all students who are 2 to 5 grades below their grade level. The design of the school can be arranged so that all students are placed in knowledge-based learning groups for math, reading and writing of no more than 6-10 students.

Teachers in grades K-2, 3-5, and 6-8, are responsible for all the students in their respective grades for three years, working together for the success of all the students, i, e., three small schools within a school.

Twice a week for two hours the school divides the students in Family Groups of no more than 10-12 students from multi-grades, who meet to learn the core skills research indicates children living in prolonged stress seems to need because of the brain damage.

When classroom educators, parents and school leaders better understood how children and teenager's brains are affected by living in prolonged poverty, experiencing prolonged stress and poor nutrition, they may alter their teaching strategies and child rearing practices to assist students overcome some of the damage to their brain.

APPENDIX F
--THE STRUCTURE OF THE BRAIN

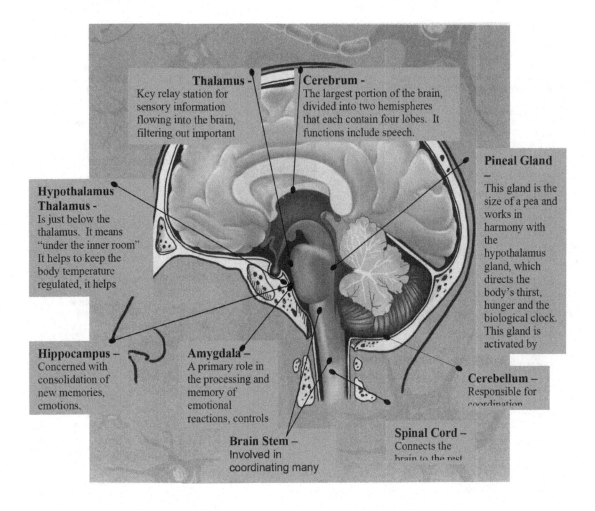

Thalamus -
Key relay station for sensory information flowing into the brain, filtering out important

Cerebrum -
The largest portion of the brain, divided into two hemispheres that each contain four lobes. It functions include speech.

Pineal Gland –
This gland is the size of a pea and works in harmony with the hypothalamus gland, which directs the body's thirst, hunger and the biological clock. This gland is activated by

Hypothalamus Thalamus -
Is just below the thalamus. It means "under the inner room" It helps to keep the body temperature regulated, it helps

Hippocampus –
Concerned with consolidation of new memories, emotions.

Amygdala –
A primary role in the processing and memory of emotional reactions, controls

Cerebellum –
Responsible for coordination

Brain Stem –
Involved in coordinating many

Spinal Cord –
Connects the brain to the rest

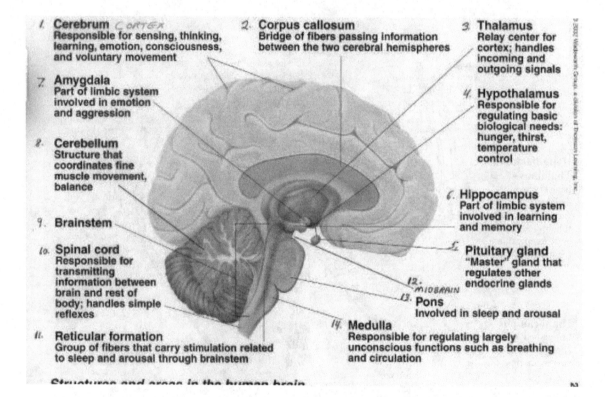

1. **Cerebrum** *CORTEX*
Responsible for sensing, thinking, learning, emotion, consciousness, and voluntary movement

7. **Amygdala**
Part of limbic system involved in emotion and aggression

8. **Cerebellum**
Structure that coordinates fine muscle movement, balance

9. **Brainstem**

10. **Spinal cord**
Responsible for transmitting information between brain and rest of body; handles simple reflexes

11. **Reticular formation**
Group of fibers that carry stimulation related to sleep and arousal through brainstem

2. **Corpus callosum**
Bridge of fibers passing information between the two cerebral hemispheres

3. **Thalamus**
Relay center for cortex; handles incoming and outgoing signals

4. **Hypothalamus**
Responsible for regulating basic biological needs: hunger, thirst, temperature control

6. **Hippocampus**
Part of limbic system involved in learning and memory

5. **Pituitary gland**
"Master" gland that regulates other endocrine glands

12. MIDBRAIN

13. **Pons**
Involved in sleep and arousal

14. **Medulla**
Responsible for regulating largely unconscious functions such as breathing and circulation

Structures and areas in the human brain

APPENDIX G
-- DATA DRIVEN INSTRUCTION

Scantron Ed Performance results are categorized as follows: below average, low average, high average, and above average, based on fall and winter assessments. A decrease in the 'below average' category is considered a gain in achievement, while decreases in the other categories may not necessarily indicate a decline in achievement. Conversely, any increase in the 'above average' category would signify improved achievement.

The data charts below illustrate the percentage of students scoring in each of the four categories across reading, mathematics, and science. The assessment objectives and test items are aligned with the Michigan GLCEs and are broken down by teacher and class. The results include an item-analysis that enables the administration and faculty to identify students' deficiencies and refocus instruction and strategies to address specific objectives

SCANTRON EDUCATION PERFORMANCE RESULTS: FALL 2011 – WINTER 2012, TOTAL SCHOOLWIDE RESULTS

Total Students Tested: Fall 2011 = 136/365;   Winter 2012 = 327/365

SCHOOLWIDE	Above Average		High Average		Low Average		Below Average	
2011 – 2012	Fall %	Winter %	Fall %	Winter %	Fall %	Winter %	Fall %	Winter %
READING	1	2	10	15	31	28	57	54
MATHEMATICS	0	2	6	9	19	28	75	64

Schoolwide, students demonstrated incremental gains in every category. Specifically, 3% of students moved up from both the below average and low average categories, resulting in a 6% increase in the above average and high average categories. In mathematics, while the gains were minimal, there was incremental growth across all categories, with 9% of students in the lowest category showing an increase in achievement, as reflected by improved scores across the three higher categories ED. ED. PERFORMANCE PERCENT OF STUDENTS SCORING IN EACH ACHIEVEMENT CATEGORY

	Reading 2011 – 2012	Above Average %		High Average %		Low Average %		Below Average %	
	Grade Level	Fall	Winter	Fall	Winter	Fall	Winter	Fall	Winter
+	2nd	5	3	11	21	32	23	53	54
-	3rd	3	5	12	10	28	16	59	71
+	4th	5	3	10	9	25	37	62	51
-	5th	0	0	12	8	20	32	69	61
+	6th	2	7	15	14	24	21	60	59
+	7th	3	0	11	17	27	37	59	46
+	8th	3	0	8	31	31	31	57	39
-	9th	0	0	11	7	28	41	61	52

(+ indicates gain in achievement; - indicates decline in achievement).

The categories 'above average' and 'high average' correlate to proficiency. While some grade levels showed gains in reading achievement at the lowest levels, they also experienced a decline in scores at the upper levels. Grades 3 and 6 showed an increase in the highest achievement category by 2% and 5%, respectively. However, Grade 3 also reflects a significant increase in the number of students scoring in the lowest category by 12%, which is concerning.

It appears that those scoring in the 'low average' category on the fall assessment declined to 'below average' in January. In the 'high average' category, Grades 2, 7, and 8 reflect an increase. Notably, Grade 8 posted a 23% gain in students scoring at 'high average,' although the percentage of students at 'above average' declined from 3% to 0%. This group showed an encouraging decline in the percentage of students in the 'below average' category by 18%. Grade 6 also saw a 5% gain in the 'above average' category, with slight improvements in other categories.

Grade 2 indicates an overall increase in achievement, with 9% of students scoring 'low average' in the fall moving up to 'above average' in the winter. However, there is a slight decline in achievement in the lowest category (1%) and the highest category (2%). Grade 9 posts a net gain of 5%, with a 4% decline in scores at 'above average,' yet showing a significant 9% improvement in 'below average' students moving up to 'low average.'

ED PERFORMANCE PERCENT OF STUDENTS SCORING IN EACH ACHIEVEMENT CATEGORY

	Math 2011 – 2012	Above Average %		High Average %		Low Average %		Below Average %	
	Grade Level	Fall	Winter	Fall	Winter	Fall	Winter	Fall	Winter
+	2nd	0	0	14	20	21	21	67	59
+	3rd	0	5	9	7	29	19	62	69
-	4th	5	0	3	9	16	15	77	77
-	5th	0	0	5	2	17	21	79	78
+	6th	0	2	7	4	25	44	68	50

+	7th	0	0	8	9	22	34	69	56
+	8th	0	6	0	8	20	22	80	64
+	9th	0	7	0	11	19	22	81	59

(+ indicates gain in achievement; - indicates decline in achievement). In the chart above, Grades 2, 3, 6, 7, 8, and 9 showed improvement in student achievement in Mathematics, with Grades 8 and 9 demonstrating significant gains in all categories. These grades increased from 0% in the two highest categories to a combined increase of 14% for Grade 8 and 18% for Grade 9. Grade 2 reflects systemic change indicative of differentiated instruction.

There is incremental growth among both low and high-achieving students. Grade 3 results reflect marked improvement; while the 'high average' category decreased, it is apparent that a percentage of these students moved up to 'above average.' Math results for Grade 4 reflect no growth for the lowest-achieving students, and it appears that the highest-achieving students declined as well, with only 1% of the students moving up from 'low average' to 'high average.'

Grade 5 showed a decline in achievement, with 5% of students scoring at 'high average' in the fall assessment and a 3% decline in winter. Grade 6 experienced an overall gain in achievement among the lowest-achieving category, with 18% of 'below average' students moving up to 'low average,' which increased by 19%. One percent of students scoring in 'high average' declined to 'low average,' while 2% showed an increase to 'above average,' which is significant.

REFERENCES

Bernhardt, V. L. (2004). Data analysis for continuous school improvement (2nd ed.). Larchmont, NY: Eye on Education. [available at http://www.eyeoneducation.com]

Black, P., & Wiliam, D. (1998). Inside the black box: Raising standards through classroom assessment. Phi Delta Kappan, 80(2), 139-148. [available at http://www.pdkintl.org/kappan/kbla9810.htm]

DuFour, R., Eaker, R., & DuFour, R. (Eds.). (2005). On common ground: The power of professional learning communities. Bloomington, IN: National Educational Service. [available at http://www.nesonline.com]

Schmoker, M. (1999). Results: The key to continuous school improvement (2nd ed.). Alexandria, VA: Association for Supervision and Curriculum Development. [particularly pages 1-55; available at http://shop.ascd.org]

Supovitz, J. A., & Klein, V. (2003). Mapping a course for improved student learning: How innovative schools systematically use student permeance data to guide improvement. Philadelphia, PA. [available at http://www.cpre.org/Publications/AC-08.pdf

Data Driven Teaching

Bernhardt, V. L. (2004). Data analysis for continuous school improvement (2nd ed.). Larchmont, NY: Eye on Education. [available at http://www.eyeoneducation.com]

Black, P., & Wiliam, D. (1998). Inside the black box: Raising standards through classroom assessment. Phi Delta Kappan, 80(2), 139-148. [available at http://www.pdkintl.org/kappan/kbla9810.htm]

DuFour, R., Eaker, R., & DuFour, R. (Eds.). (2005). On common ground: The power of professional learning communities. Bloomington, IN: National Educational Service. [available at http://www.nesonline.com]

Schmoker, M. (1999). Results: The key to continuous school improvement (2nd ed.). Alexandria, VA: Association for Supervision and Curriculum Development. [particularly pages 1-55; available at http://shop.ascd.org]

Supovitz, J. A., & Klein, V. (2003). Mapping a course for improved student learning: How innovative schools systematically use student performance data to guide improvement. Philadelphia, PA. [available at http://www.cpre.org/Publications/AC-08.pdf].

Effective Teachers in Urban Communities

Brophy, J. 1999. Teaching, Educational practices series 1. Geneva, Switzerland: International Bureau of Education.

Diffily, D., and H. Perkins. 2002. Preparing to teach in urban schools: Advice from urban teachers. Teacher Education and Practice: The Journal of the Texas Association of Colleges for Teacher Education 15(1/2): 57–73.

Dunlap, K. 2004. Exercise in classroom warms up kids' minds. The Arizona Republic, November 27.

Guyton, E. 1994. First year teaching experiences of early childhood urban teachers. Paper presented at the Annual Meeting of the American Educational Research Association, April 4–8, New Orleans. ERIC ED 369 856.

Haberman, M. 1995a. Star teachers of children in poverty. West Lafayette, IN: Kappa Delta Pi, International Honor Society in Education.

Haberman, M. 1995b. Selecting 'star' teachers for children and youth in urban poverty. Phi Delta Kappan 76(10): 777–81.

Honig, M. I., J. Kahne, and M. W. McLaughlin. 2001. School-community connections: Strengthening opportunity to learn and opportunity to teach. In Handbook of research on teaching, 4th ed., ed. V. Richardson, 998–1028. Washington, DC: American Educational Research Association.

Kossan, P. 2003. Best bets: Teachers who defy the odds. The Arizona Republic, November 27.

Murrell, P. C., Jr. 2001. The community teacher: A new framework for effective urban teaching. New York: Teachers College Press.

Olmedo, I. M. 1997. Challenging old assumptions: Preparing teachers for inner city schools. Teaching and Teacher Education 13(3): 245–58.

Olson, L. 2003. The great divide. Education Week 22(17): 9–18.

Quartz, K. 2003. 'Too angry to leave:' Supporting new teachers' commitment to transform urban schools. Journal of Teacher Education 54(2):99–111.

Sparks, C. 2004. Making school a 2nd home. The Arizona Republic, November 29. Tredway, L. 1999.

The art of juggling: Preparing preservice teachers for urban schools. Journal of Negro Education 68(3): 382–96.

Warren, S. R. 2002. Stories from the classroom: How expectations and efficacy of diverse teachers affect the academic performance of children in poor urban schools. Educational Horizons 80(3): 109–16.

Weiner, L. 1993. Preparing teachers for urban schools. New York: Teachers College Press.

Weiner, L. 1999. Urban teaching: The essentials. New York

Mindfulness

ANT-C: Rueda, M.R., Fan, J., McCandliss, B.D., Halparin, J.D.,

Attentional Networks in Childhood Neuropsychological, 42, 1029 1040.

Black, D. S. & Fernando, R. (2013). Mindfulness Training and Classroom Behavior Among Lower-income and Ethnic Minority

Elementary School Children. Journal of Child and Family Studies.

Black, D.S., Milam, J., and Sussman, S. (2009).

Sitting-Meditation Interventions Among Youth: A Review of Treatment Efficacy. Pediatrics 124, 532-541.

Burke, C. (2010). Mindfulness-Based Approaches with Children and Adolescents: A Preliminary Review of Current Research in an

Emergent Field. Journal of Child Family Studies, 19:2, 133-144.

CAMM: Greco, Laurie A.; Baer, Ruth A.; Smith, Gregory T. (2011) Assessing Mindfulness in Children and Adolescents: Development and Validation of the Child and Adolescent Mindfulness Measure (CAMM). Psychological Assessment, 23:3, 606-614.

Davidson, R.J. and Sharon Begley, The Emotional Life of Your Brain, Hudson St. Press, New York, 2012.

Doidge, N. The Brain That Changes Itself, Penguin, NY, 2007.

Fields, R.D. The Other Brain, Simon and Schuster, New York, 2010.

Flook, L. et al. (2010). Effects of Mindful Awareness Practices on Executive Functions in Elementary School Children. Journal of Applied School Psychology, 26:1, 70-95.

Hanson, R. and R. Mendius, Buddha's Brain, New Harbinger, Oakland, CA, 2009.

Horstman, J. The Scientific American Day in the Life of Your Brain. Jossey-bass/Wiley & Sons, San Francisco, 2009.

Horstman, Judith, (2013), Mindfulness in Public Schools, Building Wellness & Resilience in Our Children, A Manual for Teaching Mindfulness, Complied by the South Burlington, Vermont, School District.

Jennings, P. A. (2012). Building an Evidence Base for Mindfulness in Educational Settings. http://www.mindful.org/mindful-voices/on-education/building-an-evidence-base-for-mindfulness-in-educational-settings

Jennings, P. A. et al. (2011). Improving Classroom Learning Environments by Cultivating Awareness and Resilience in Education (CARE): Results of Two Pilot Studies. Journal of Classroom Interaction, 46:1, 37-48.

Kinder Associates, Behavioral Rubric: Kinder, R. & Kinder, M. www.mindfulyoga.com

MAAS: Brown, K.W. & Ryan, R.M. (2003). The Benefits of Being Present: Mindfulness and Its Role in Psychological Well-Being. Journal of Personality and Social Psychology, 84, 822-848.

ProQOL: Stamm, B., 2009. Professional Quality of Life: Compassion Satisfaction and Fatigue Version 5 (ProQOL). www.proqol.org

Rechtschaffen, Daniel, The Way of Mindful Education, Cultivating Well-Being in Teachers and Students, (2014), W. W. Norton and Company, New York.

Siegal, Daniel J. The Mindful Brain, Norton, NY, 2007.

Smith, A. Guzman-Alvarez, A., Westover, T., Keller, S., & Fuller, S. (2012). Mindful Schools Program Evaluation. University of California at Davis: Center for Education and Evaluation Services.

TSES: Tschannen-Moran, M., & Woolfolk Hoy, A. (2001). Teacher Efficacy: Capturing an Elusive Construct. Teaching and Teacher Education, 17, 783-805

School Turnarounds

Brinson, D., Kowal, J., & Hassel, B. (2008). School turnarounds: Actions and results. Lincoln, IL: Center on Innovation & Improvement. Retrieved from www.centerii.org

Davis, Lou. (1966). "The Design of Jobs." Industrial Relations, 6:21-45.

DuFour, Richard, DuFour, Rebecca, Eaker, Robert, Karhanek, Gayle, (2004). Whatever It Takes: How Professional Learning

Communities Respond When Kids Don't Learn. Solution Tree, Bloomington, IN.

Duke, D.L. (2006). "Keys to Sustaining Successful School Turnarounds." ERS Spectrum, Education Research Service 24 (4) Retrieved from http://www.darden.edu/uploadedFiles/Centers_of_Excellence/PLE/KeysToSuccess.pdf

Eaker, Robert; DuFour, Richard; Burnette, Rebecca , Getting Started: Recurlturing Schools To Become Professional Learning Communities. National Educational Service, Bloomington, IN, BKF00120: Web site:

Evans, G W, (2004), "The Environment of Childhood Poverty." American Psychologist. 59 (2), 77-92.

Gunnar, M.R., Frenn, K. Wewerka, S.S., & Van Ryzin, M.J., (2009); Miller, A.L., Seifer, R., Stroud, L., S.J., Sheinkopf, & Dickstein, S., (2006).

"Behavioral Indices of Emotion Regulation Related to School Attitudes, Motivation, and Behavior Problems in a Low-Income Preschool Sample" Annals of the New York Academy of Sciences, 1094, 325-329.

Hess, F and Gift, T., (February 2009), "School Turnarounds: Resisting the Hype, Giving Them Hope." Education Outlook.

Richard Walton, Organizational Life Cycle

Robert Marzano (2001); Classroom Instruction that Works: Research-based Strategies for Increasing Student Achievement. ASCD

Smarick, A., (October 2009), "The Turnaround Fallacy," Education Next.

Articles published in *Brain World,* Warrington and Brenda Parker, *"Happy Teachers, Happy Students," "The United Nations Declaration, On the Universal Rights of Education for all Children,"" Bullying and the Impact on Children Brains."*

Printed in the United States
by Baker & Taylor Publisher Services